An Economic History of Ancient India
(300 B.C. – A.D. 700)

About the Author

Professor M.L. Bose taught in the Dibrugarh University for nearly thirty years and had contributed more than thirty papers in Regional and National Seminars and Journals of repute. An Aurobindite Prof. Bose guided many research scholars for their Ph.D. research. His earlier published works, namely: *Historical and Constitutional Documents of North-East India, British Policy in the North-East Frontier Agency, Development of Administration in Assam, Social History of Assam, Social and Cultural History of Arunachal Pradesh, Social and Cultural History of Ancient India* (2nd edn.), were very well received in the academic world.

AN ECONOMIC HISTORY OF ANCIENT INDIA (300 B.C. – A.D. 700)

M.L. Bose

CONCEPT PUBLISHING COMPANY PVT. LTD.
NEW DELHI - 110 059

ISBN-13: 978-93-88937-55-9 (HB)
ISBN-13: 978-93-88937-56-6 (PB)

First Published 2020

Published and Printed by

Concept Since 1974

Concept Publishing Company Pvt. Ltd.
A/15-16, Commercial Block, Mohan Garden
New Delhi-110059 (India)
T: 25351460, 25351794, *F*: 091-11-25357109
E: publishing@conceptpub.com, W: www.conceptpub.com

Cataloging in Publication Data--Courtesy: D.K. Agencies (P) Ltd. <docinfo@dkagencies.com>

Bose, Manilal, author.
An economic history of ancient India (300 B.C. – A.D. 700) / M.L. Bose.
pages cm
Includes bibliographical references and index.
ISBN 9789388937559 (HB)
ISBN 9789388937566 (PB)

1. India--Economic conditions--To 1000. 2. India--History--324 B.C.-1000 A.D.
I. Title.

LCC HC434.B67 2020 | DDC 330.934 23

In Memory of my father

Late Sisir Kumar Bose

PREFACE

Initially the Economic History of India begins with the Indus Valley Civilization (3300-1300 B.C.), whose economy appears to have depended significantly on trade and examples of overseas trade, notable being Indus-Mesopotamia relations. Actually the Vedic period saw countable units of precious metal being used for exchange. And the term *Nishka* appears in this sense in the *Ṛgveda*. A significant development, later Vedic period began codifying the ancient Indian population based on caste, a social stratification which created a hierarchy of priests (*Brahmins*), warriors (*Kshatriyas*), merchants (*Vaishyas*) and labourers (*Shudra*).

Around 600 B.C., the Mahajanapadas minted punch-marked silver coins. And the period was marked by intensive trade activity and urban development. By 300 B.C., the Maurya Empire had geopolitically united most of the Indian subcontinent. Thus the resulting political unity and military security allowed for a common economic system and enhanced trade and commerce, with increased agricultural productivity.

As per historical chronology, the Maurya Empire was followed by classical and early mediaeval kingdoms, including the Guptas, Cholas. Western Gangas, Palas, Harsha, Rashtrakutas and Hoysalas.

It is to be remembered that ancient India had a significant urban population, much of India's population resided in villages, whose economy was largely isolated and self-sustaining. Agriculture was the predominant occupation, mainly growing wheat, barley and peas and was content with a village's food requirements besides providing raw materials for hand-based industries, such as textile, food processing and crafts. And apart from farmers, people worked as barbers, carpenters, *vaidyas*, goldsmiths and weavers like vocations.

It is pertinent to note that an authentic economic history of ancient India can be reconstructed on the basis of information churned out of various sources, e.g. foreign accounts, religious literatures — religious and secular, epigraphic records, land grants, numismatic sources and archaeological finds etc.

This book is devised as an introductory text for post-graduate students of various Indian universities. Written in simple language and supported by facts and figures, the entire information is gathered under the following chapters in elaborate manner: Introduction, Agrarian relations, Agriculture, Gardening and Cattle farming, Arts and Crafts, Trade and Commerce, Guilds and Partnerships, Labour, Currency and Credit, and Revenue and Expenditure etc.

I do hope, like my other books like *Social and Cultural History of India*, this will also prove useful and informative to all those for whom this is meant.

I express my gratefulness to different scholars, my colleagues and friends, and students. At the same time I am thankful to publisher for undertaking publication of this book.

M.L. Bose

CONTENTS

SANSKRIT ALPHABETS AND ITS PRONUNCIATION

Vowels	*Short*	*Long*
guttural	a	ā
palatal	i	ī
labial	u	ū
retro flex	r	r̄

Consonants	*Unvoiced*	*Unvoiced Aspirate*	*Voiced*	*Voiced Aspirate*	*Nasal*
guttural	k	kh	g	gh	ń
palatal	c	ch	j	jh	n
retro flex	t	th	d	dh	n
dental	ṭ	th	d	dh	ṅ
labial	p	ph	b	bh	m

Anusvara	ṁ
visarga	ḥ

Sibilants	
palatal	ś
retro flex	ṣ
dental	s
aspiration	h

ABBREVIATIONS

A.M.S.J.	Ashutosh Mukherjee Silver Jubilee Commermorative Volumes
B.R.S.	British Revenue System of U.N. Ghosal
E.I.	Epigraphia Indica
J.A.S.B.	Journal of Asiatic Society of Bengal
I.A.	Indian Antiquary

1

Introduction

Indian civilization developed into that what is called *Wonder that was India* by A.L. Basham, between 6th century B.C. and A.D. 7th century. It cast off its prehistoric shed and entered into the ancient historic period and ushered into an era of great creativity which found expression in art, architecture, literature and philosophy. But all these treasures of Indian civilization could flourish on an economic background.

The intellectual concept of Indian body politic was made a political reality after the invasion of Alexander of Macedonia. On the ruins of the political fabric in North India, the Mauryas established an empire on the Indian subcontinent and the focus of historic development shifted to the Ganga valley from the Indus. The political stability and efficient administration provided a milieu of law and order which encouraged the growth of agriculture, arts and crafts, trades and business, intellectual ferment and philosophical speculation which made India great in the world history. The Mauryan political fabric which collapsed at the end of pre-Christian era, was partially restored by the Kuṣaṇas, and with an interregnum of the *Śuṅga-Kāṅva* periods, the Imperial Guptas raised the imperial standard once again and Indian culture flourished into its classical form. All these developments were possible as already remarked above, because of her wealth. It is the purpose of this work to provide a survey of this economic activity.

I have written a very short compendium on *Social and Cultural History of Ancient India* which was published in 1989. The first edition of the book becomes out of stock and the second edition with a little alteration and addition of one more chapter is now published by Concept Publishing Company. Its demand in the market proved that though there are many works on this subject, a small book dealing with the subject was a necessity.

Similar conclusion may be drawn regarding the necessity of a small book on the *Economic History of Ancient India*. These are quite a few scholarly works on the subject, *viz. Buddhist India* by Rhys Davis, *Social and Rural Economy of Northern India* by A.N. Bose, *Economic Condition of Ancient India* by Pran Nath, *Economic Life and Progress of Ancient India* by Bandopadhyaya, *Corporate Life in Ancient India* by R.K. Mookerji, *Ancient India* by E.J. Rapson, besides *Cambridge History of India*, Vol. I by the same author, which are the pioneering works in the study of socio-economic life of ancient India. But these works deal with mainly the pre-classical period and are mostly based on Buddhist literature, Greek-Roman sources, the *Smṛtis*, Kauṭilya's *Arthaśāstra* and the two epics. Moreover none of these works are now available in new academic institutions, for almost none of these books are available in the market.

Now the students of many universities wish to study ancient *Indian Economic History* in their post-graduate course. But, they do not get a text book by reading which they can get a connected history of economic life of Ancient India. The works like *The Age of Imperial Unity: The Classical Age*, both published by Bharatiya Vidya Bhavan, *The New History of the Indian People* by R.C. Majumdar and also the books by A.S. Altekar. *A Comprehensive History of India* published by India History Congress, A.L. Basham's *Wonder that was India: Economic Life of Northern India* by L. Gopal, *Economic by Early India (200 B.C. - A.D. 300)* by Adhya, *Life in the Gupta Age* by B.A. Saletore are scholarly works, but do not serve the purpose of a text book for the post-graduate students. Therefore, I undertook to write the present work providing references to the several works existing on this subject and on the basis of information found in the existing books.

It may be necessary to provide an idea of the sources of data for the study of this subject, for many may intend to study the original sources for their satisfaction. Therefore, outline of the original sources are given below:

For the pre-Mauryan and Mauryan period, a lot of information can be obtained from early Greek writers. These are translated into English by J.W. McCrindle. His works like *Ancient India as described by Megasthenes and Arrian, Ancient India as described by Ptolemy, Ancient India as described in Classical Literature* and *The Periplus of Erythrean Sea* translated by W.H. Schoff provide first hand account on the ports of India and the trade of ancient India with the Western world. *The Christian Topography of Cosmas (A.D. 6th Century)* provides information on geography and commerce of India and Śri Lanka. *Procopius of Caesarea* supplements the information contained in the accounts of Cosmas. The observations of Nearchus and *Law Digest* of Justinian supply ample idea on economic conditions and trade and industry of India as well.

Besides the Greeks, we have some information from the tour diary of Fa-hien, Hiuen-Tsang and I-tsing. the English translation of S. Beal of *Life of Hiuen-Tsang* by Sharmans Hwui Li and Yen Tsung from Chinese, and T. Walter's on *Yuan Chwang's Travels in India* in two volumes, provide much information on the economic life of ancient India. Though in many cases they are untrustworthy, still we can glean some data on economic activities in ancient India.

Besides these foreign account, we have indigenous literature both religious and secular which give us lot of information on the economic life. The *Ṛg Veda*, the two epics the *Rāmāyaṇa* and the *Mahābhārata*, the several *Smṛtis* of Gautama, Manu, Yājñavalkya, Bṛhaspati and Nārada, and astronomical works of Varāhamihira entitled *Bṛhatsaṁhita*, the lexicon *Amarkoṣa* provide information on ownership of land, agriculture and agricultural products, gardening, animal husbandry, trade and commerce, currency and credit, revenue system, business organization, labour etc. Kāmaṇdaka and Śukra's works are useful for collecting data on revenue system of the period. Moreover, the literary works of Śudraka, Kālidāsa, Daṇdi etc. provide useful data for the study of geography, trade and commerce of ancient India.

Also we have epigraphic records inscribed on stone or copper plates. E. Hultzsch's *Inscriptions of Aśoka*, J.F. Fleet's *Inscriptions of Early Gupta Kings and Their Successors, Epigraphia Indica* composed by various editors, D.C. Sircar's *Select Inscriptions Bearing on Indian History and Civilization* provide a lot of information on economic life. The epigraphic records inscribed on stone or copper plates can be fruitfully utilized for writing economic history of ancient India. We get information regarding agrarian expansions, ownership of land, rate of productivity, relation between agriculture and crafts, fragmentation or consolidation of holdings, extension of the money economy. There besides land grants, also enumerate fiscal dues transferred to donees by some terms like *hiraṇya, udranga, uparikara, bāli, bhoga, bhoga-bhāga* etc.

Grants also provide data on agrarian rights such as those to pastures, irrigation facilities, river, trees, hills etc. We can study the problem of ownership of land and see whether it was collective or individual.

Grants may provide information regarding organization of agricultural production; agricultural resources and products are mentioned in many grants. Chandela grants show cotton, sugarcane, hemp were important cash corps in central India. The land grants of Assam mention useful trees like blackberry, mango, red-silk, cotton tree etc. Chandela and Gahadavala grants mention iron and salt as the main produce of the land. Land grants mention *arahattas* or Persian wheels were used in India for irrigation or mode of irrigation from well, tank etc.

Sātvāhana grants mention *nivartana* as unit of land measurement. Gupta grants too provide information on unit of land measurement.

From Land grants, we know that revenue was estimated in terms of money in Bengal and Orissa. Land grants are also useful for the history of the towns as well as economic activities in them. Thus agriculture and agrarian relations, irrigation system, crafts and industries, trade and commerce, currency and credit, revenue system can be studied by a careful study of epigraphic sources.

The numismatic sources throw important side lights on the economic life of ancient India. A lot of punchmark coins, coins of Indo-Greeks, Romans, Kuṣaṇas, Śaka Kṣatrapas, Guptas and others have been found in different parts of the country. The art of coining was an important occupation and helped the development of metallic industry. The coins served as medium of exchange. These must have facilitated the growth of industry and trade.

The archaeological finds throw a lot of light on the developments of arts and crafts of ancient India. The shards and potteries of Ahichhatra and Kauśambī, the terra-cotta finds throw an important light on the economic history of ancient India together with her cultural developments. These have not only unearthed the articrafts but have exhibited the skill of architects, sculptors and painters of the period.

Thus, by a careful study of literature, both foreign and indigenous, epigraphs and currency as also the archaeological finds. Besides the secondary sources mentioned above, one can study the economic life of ancient Indian people.

1st August, 1996 **M.L. Bose**
Dibrugarh, Assam

2

GEOGRAPHICAL BACKGROUND

History of a country is largely influenced by its climatic conditions. These to a great extent mould and shape the life and activities of the people and their culture. Therefore, the study of geography is necessary for a proper understanding of man's economic life.

Situated between 8° and 37° north latitude and 66° and 99° east longitude with an area of one million and a half square miles comprising high mountain ranges, lofty plateaus, extensive plains, sandy deserts, large rivers, fertile river valleys, and forests of every descriptions, India can be divided into three well-marked regions[1], *viz.*,

(i) The *Himālayan* regions in the north;
(ii) The great plains of the Indo-Gangetic valley; and
(iii) The Deccan plateau.

The *Himālayas* which run in a south-east curve all along the northern front of India and separates it from the plateau of Tibet, include several parallel ranges of lofty mountains, with deep valleys between them. They cover a region about 1500 miles long and 150 to 200 miles in breadth containing about 114 peaks of over 20,000 feet. It holds within its arms two mighty rivers whose southern bends from the western and eastern limits of the greatest mountain ranges in the world.[2]

Nearly 200 miles long and 150 to 200 miles broad, two extensive plains formed by the *Indus* and the *Gangā* and the *Brahmaputra* with their tributaries and affluents were the seats of early civilization of India.[3] These plains witnessed the rise and fall of the great empires like the Mauryas and the Guptas. From the valleys of these rivers, Indian civilization radiated in different directions. The *Indus*, which gave its name to India, helped to develop the earliest civilization of India. More than 2000 years before the birth of Christ, the valleys of the river with its tributaries — the *Jhelum, Chenab, Ravi, Beas* and *Sutlej* had developed a high culture known as Soan culture which spread as far as the sea and along the western sea coast as far as Gujarāt.[4]

The basin of *Indus* is divided from that of *Gangā* by the Thar desert of Rājasthan and by a range of low hills. The western part of this *Gangā* plain, from the region around Delhi to Patnā, including the *doab*, the land between the *Gangā* and its greatest tributary *Jamunā*, has been the heart of India. Here on this plain known as *Āryavarta*, the land of *Āryans*, a classical culture was formed. At its north in Bengal, the *Gangā* forms a large delta; here the *Brahamapūtra* which flows through Tibet by the way of the valley of Assam, the eastern most outpost of *Hindu* culture, joins the *Gangā*.[5]

The influence of geography is very clearly marked on the Deccan, usually described as a peninsula washed by the ocean on all sides except one. It is in the form of an immense triangle which rests on the *Vindhya* range as its base and terminates in Cape of Comorin as its vertex. On the west, an almost unbroken range called *Mālābār* Hills faces the Arabian Sea and to the east lies south-west the Eastern *Ghāts* facing the Bay of Bengal. The coast line between Eastern *Ghāts* and the Bay of Bengal is usually known as the Coromandal coast. From the sea the *Mālābār* Hills recedes 40 miles; it is precipitous. Towards the land its slope is always gradual and is occasionally imperceptible. On both sides, it is clothed with magnificent timber.[6]

The Eastern *Ghāts* is less elevated and is a tamper range. Its loftiest summits are not above 3000 feet. Its distance from the sea is considerable and the descent is seldom abrupt.[7] In its course southwards instead of being continued to extremity, it stops about midway, and turning gradually south-west meets with a traverse range called the *Nilgiri* Hills which have summits exceeding 7000 feet and by which it becomes linked with the Western *Ghāts*.[8]

The Deccan triangle with sides composed of mountain ranges, is formed with that of the Deccan and an elevated table land, which has a gradual but continuous slope eastward from the Western *Ghāts* to the sea.[9] It is noted for its black soils which are the best suited for growing deep rooted crops, especially cotton.

In accordance with this slope, all the rivers of any magnitude: the *Mahānandā*, the *Godāvarī*, the *Kṛṣṇā*, the *Pennār*, the *Palar*, the *Kāverī* carry the drainage to the Bay of Bengal. This table land cannot boast the fertility of the basin of the *Gangā*, because while it is exposed to a more scorching heat, it has no river fed by perpetual snow. The torrents of rain, however, which periodically descent on the Western *Ghāts* compensate in some degree this defect and provide the means of a system of irrigation, which carried on by collecting the superfluous water in immense tanks during the rainy season, at one time made the Deccan proverbial for beauty and productiveness.[10]

The south-eastern part of the peninsula forms a large plain known as *Tāmil* country, the culture of which was once independent and is not yet completely united with that of the north.

2.1 Meteorology

The most factor in the meteorology of India is the influence of the monsoon which is written large in the history of India.[11] The south-west monsoon highly charged with humidity, is a continuation of south-east trade wind. It passes across India from June to September and retreats between October to December. It is divided into two currents, one moves up the Bay of Bengal, the other up the Arabian Sea. Part of the Bay of Bengal current is deflected to Burma but the main current proceeds over eastern Bengal and Assam. It is deflected by the *Himālayas* westward across the *Gangā* plain to the hills of the north-west. The Arabian Sea current strikes the Western Ghats where it causes heavy rainfall. The valley of *Narmadā* and *Tāptī* are the gateways through which the monsoon finds across to the states of Central India. It passes over the sandy deserts of Rājasthan until it meets the deflected the Bay of Bengal current over the eastern Punjāb. The full strength of this monsoon lasts for about three months. From the third week of September, these two currents retreat from northern India and by the end of October, pass of the country.

The north-east monsoon, which is sometimes referred to as the south-west monsoon in retreat blows from the middle of October to the end of December and becomes hotter and drier as the spring advances. The south-east coast of Madras, however, is watered by both the eastern and the south-west monsoon and the north-east monsoon between October and December. But north-west India is subject to a succession of shallow storms from January to March and the *Gangā* plain receives slight winter rain and considerable spring rain.

The normal annual rain-fall varied from 460 inches in Assam to less than 3 inches in Rajasthan in the past. The prosperity of India depends much on the success or failure of the monsoon; though some measures are taken to remedy the consequences of this monsoon by construction of wells, tanks, dykes and canals for irrigation purposes.

2.2 Climatic Conditions

From Kāshmīr in the north to the Cape of Comorin in the south, the subcontinent is about 2000 miles long and therefore, its climate varies considerably.[12] The *Himālaya* region has cold winter, with frost and snow. In the northern plains, the winter is cool, with wide variation in night and day temperatures whereas the summer season is intolerable. The temperature of Deccan varies less with the season, though in the higher parts of the plateau nights are cool in winter.[13] The *Tāmil* plain is continuously hot, but its temperature never rises to that of the northern plains in summer.[14]

Many other ancient civilizations, such as those of Greeks, Romans and the Chinese had to contend with hard winter. India, on the other hand, was blessed with a bounteous nature which demanded little of men in return for sustenance.[15]

REFERENCES

1. *Cambridge History of India*, Vol. I, reprint, 1978.
2. *The Vedic Age*, pp. 91-94.
3-5. A.L. Basham, *The Wonder that was India*, 3rd revised edn., London, 1967, pp. 1-2.
6-11. *Cambridge History of India*, Vol. I, pp. 5-6.
11. C.C. Davis, *An Historical Atlas of Indian Peninsula*, 2nd edition, 1961, pp. 77-78.
12-15. A.L. Basham, *op. cit.*, pp. 2-3.

3

AGRARIAN RELATIONS

3.1 Land

Land is the bedrock of Indian economy and directly or indirectly not less than 80 per cent people are still dependent on it. Agriculture provides sustenance to people. Raw materials of industries, arts and crafts and articles of trade and commerce are derived from land.

3.2 Types of Land

Lands, however, are divided on the basis of their quality. The *Amarakoṣa*[1] refers to twelve types of land. They are: (a) *urvara* (fertile), (b) *ūsara* (barren), (c) *maru* (desert), (d) *aprahata* (fallow), (e) *śādvala* (grassy land), (f) *pankila* (muddy land), (g) *jalaprāyamanupam* (watery or wet land), (h) *kachha* (land contiguous to water), (i) *śarkarā* (land full of pebbles and pieces of lime stones), (j) *śarkāvati* (sandy), (k) *nadīmātṛka* (land watered from a river for cultivation), and (l) *devamātṛka* (land watered by rain). But in the inscriptions and land grants we come across such lands as (i) *kṣetra*, (ii) *khila*, (iii) *vāpi*, (iv) *apradā*, (v) *aprahata*, (vi) *vāstu*, and (vi) *gōpatha-sarah*.

The term *kṣetra* is very often recorded in inscriptions.[2] It generally means a field. But Basak and Pargiter[3] interpret *kṣetra* as cultivable field. In the *Amarakoṣa* also it is defined as a special type of land capable of producing all kinds of crops.[4]

There were, however, two types of cultivable lands, *viz.*, the dry land which required irrigation for its cultivation, and the wet land which required less water. The latter type is referred to in the Grant of Dharmaditya where the term *vapa* proceeds *kṣetra*. The term here may signify *vapi* which means a small tank, instead of *vapa* in its derivative name, meaning the field where seeds are sown.[5]

Other terms commonly met with in inscriptions are *khila* and *aprahata*. Basak explains *khila* as untilled land. This is also supported by the *Amarakoṣa*.[6]

According to McDonell and Keith, the terms *khila* and *khilya* seem to have same meaning.[7] In the opinion of Roth, the terms signify the waste land lying between cultivated fields.[8] But he admits that this meaning does not suit a verse from Ṛg Veda in which it is stated that the God places the worshipper on an unbroken *khilya* (*abhina khilya*) and he accordingly suggests the reading *akhilya-bhinne*, the land broken by barren strips. Pischel thinks that the terms denote broad lands which were used for the pasture by the community and were not broken up by cultivated fields.[9] Oldenburg, however, holds that these lands lay between cultivated fields, but need not be deemed to have been infertile, as Roth thinks.[10]

The *Nārada-smṛti*, however, clearly states that a tract of land which has not been cultivated for a year is called half-waste (*ardha-khila*) but that which has not been under cultivation for three years is called waste (*khila*) while that which has not been under cultivation for five years is no better than a forest. Thus *khila* land may be taken as a cultivable waste which was cultivated previously but is now lying uncultivated.[11]

Another term *aprahata* is mostly used in conjunction with *khila*. Basak holds that both *khila* and *aprahata* are synonymous terms signifying untilled land. But as both terms are recorded side by side in the same place, there may have been some slight technical difference in the meaning between them.[12] According to Monier Williams, *aprahata* means untilled waste.[13] Dr. Sircar defines it as "unreclaimed jungle land". Thus it appears that *khila* land is previously cultivated but now left uncultivated; and *aprahata* land is hitherto untouched by plough. Both terms can be taken together to mean cultivable waste lands.[14]

Dr. Saletore mentions another type of land which is called *aprada*.[15] He explains it as untilled land. But this suggestion does not hold good of we read carefully the passages in the inscription where it is recorded. Sometimes, it is preceded by *aprahata-khila*, sometimes by *akṣaya* (*nīvī*), *kṣetra* and *khila* only.[16] Thus, it is mentioned along with three other types of land. Basak explains it as land given to anybody else before the transaction was effected, in other words, unsettled land.[17] This seems a better explanation of *aprada* for it literally means land which is not given away. Moreover, in the section of land tenure, we shall see that this term is often connected with *dharma* (*apradadharma*) and *akṣayanīvī* etc. and have nothing to do with the types of land. It appears that the term *aprada* was generally used to this sense, rather than that suggested by Basak and Saletore.

We have reference to another type of land, called *vastu*[18] or habitable land. Monier Williams explains the word as a site for dwelling places.[19] The term is popularly used for building sites even today in India. They are generally higher than the cultivated and cultivable lands.

There was also pasture land for grazing of cattle. In the Khoh plate of Maharaja Hastin, the terms *gopath-sarah*[20] is recorded. Dr. Fleet interprets it as "the reeds grow by the cattle path."[21] This may indicate the pasture land of Nārada where the cowherds used to tend their village cattle.[22]

3.3 Ownership of Land

Be that as it may, ownership of land has remained one of the most controversial questions of ancient India history. Scholars have suggested different forms of ownership of land in ancient India and theories have not been put forward maintaining the prevalence of royal ownership, private ownership and communal ownership.

Before investigation of these theories, we should have a very clear idea about the nature of simple possession, irrespective of legal title, legal ownership and the absolute ownership. Ownership is usually defined as a quality of object to be enjoyed according to pleasure. Gautama and Manu state that attributes associated with ownership are sale, gift or mortgage and use of land according to pleasure.[23]

Now let us see how ownership is acquired. There is popular maxim that the field belongs to him who first removed the weed and the deer belongs to him who first wounded it.[24] Milindapānho also states that he who brings the land in use is called the owner of the land.[25] Possibly in the earliest time, people enjoyed the fruits of the land in many places in India without interference, though there may have been no legal title because there was plenty of land. But when the demand for land gradually increased with the progress of agriculture, the squatter's claim was certainly at stake.[26] He could no longer enjoy land merely by virtue of his first occupation without some valid title behind it. In the Gupta period, the demand for land for agriculture and other purposes was considerable. Vinegradoff rightly remarks that this maxim of Manu evidently goes back to great antiquity and it implies not permanent ownership but mere possession.[27]

Various law-givers denounce this kind of ownership by mere possession and lay down rules to give it legal validity. The earlier *Smṛtis* like Yājñavalkya's state that possession (*bhoga*) acquires validity when it is accompanied by a clear title (*agamena visudhena*) and is not valid without the same.[28] According to Bṛhaspati, possession becomes valid when it is coupled with legitimate title (*segamah*).[29] But Nārada is far more explicit regarding the legal title of ownership. Where there is enjoyment, but no title of any sort, a title is required in order to produce proprietary right.[30] Mere possession is not sufficient to create proprietary right in that case. A clear title having been produced, possession acquires validity. But possession without a clear title does not constitute evidence of ownership. He goes another step further and frames laws against illegal possession. He who can only plead possession, without being able to produce title, must be considered as thief.[31] Moreover, if a man enjoys possession without a title even for a hundred years, the ruler of the land should inflict on him the punishment ordained on a thief.[32]

Bṛhaspati and Nārada suggest, of course, another mode of valid ownership of land. He who has occupied land quite unopposed and uninterrupted for a period of thirty years, cannot be deprived of such property.[33]

The legal title of ownership might be acquired in various ways. The early law-giver, Gautama lays down that a person becomes owner (*swami*) by means of inheritance, purchase, partition, acceptance and finding.[34] Following him Manu also mentions seven lawful modes of acquiring wealth, namely inheritance, finding or friendly donation, purchase, conquest, lending at interest, performance of work (for alternatively sacrificing for others) and acceptance of a gift from the virtuous.[35]

Bṛhaspati holds that immovable property is acquired (*apyate*) in seven ways, *viz.* by learning, by purchase and mortgage, by valour, by marriage, by inheritance and by succession to the property by the kinsmen without issue.[36] Nārada further elucidates the injunctions of the former law-givers.[37] Property obtained by inheritance, gifts made in love and what has been obtained with a wife (as her dowry), these are the three sorts of pure wealth for all classes without distinction.

Thus, it appears that the earliest concept of ownership was derived from the first occupation when there were less demand for land. But in the later years, a more stable form of ownership of soil is demanded. Legal sanction was needed. Hence, the ancient jurists framed laws and regulations governing the ownership of land. These regulations duly safeguarded the interests of the possessor against a possible future challenge to the validity of the possession.

3.4 Royal Ownership

There is a story that many undertook to protect the subjects for a share of the order and herds.[38] A similar story is recorded in Buddhist theology. The *Dighanikaya* asserts that the king is entitled to half of the master of the land and ancient hoards and metals by reason of giving protection to the subjects. During the time of the Mauryas, the imperial authority was keenly felt over the major part of the Indian subcontinent. Two hundred years of continuous rule of the imperial Guptas offered a well-knit government. Their power and influence allover the empire were for the most of this period more or less unchallenged and undisputed. In such circumstances, it would not be unnatural that all lands were thought of as ultimately belonging to the kind. The supreme power was vested in the crown and individual could enjoy property quite peacefully, so long as he paid dues to the state. Thus, the tax on crops and the other products of the soil came to be looked on as a sort of rent in return of tenancy.[39]

Thus, the concept of the ultimate royal ownership of land emerged early. Manu speaks of the king as ultimate lord (*adhipati*) of the land and therefore, entitled to his share of treasure and minerals.[40] Another *Smṛti* writer, Gautama, is very clear in his opinion on the question of royal ownership, he states that the king is the master of all except *Brahmaṇas*.[41] He is supported by Bṛhaspati who declares that the king is the lord of all.[42]

Some foreign accounts substantiate royal ownership of land. Strobo holds that "The whole country belongs to the king and the farmer cultivates it for a rental in addition to paying fourth part of the produce."[43] Diodoros also agrees to the theory of royal ownership.[44] In Mauryan times, Megasthenes expressed the matter very clearly, "The second caste consists of the husbandsmen. . . . They devote the whole of their time to tillage. . . . They pay a land tribute to the king, because all India is the property of the crown and no private person is permitted to own land. Beside the land tribute, they pay into the royal treasure a fourth part of the produce of the soil."[45] These references leave no room for doubt that at least from the Maurya period onwards the supreme authority of the crown had extended over all lands.

The ownership of land by the king can also be substantiated from a host of Gupta inscriptions[46], in which the kings of this period are recorded as endowing a village or a certain amount of land. It is difficult to account for the king's power to grant rights over villages to religious bodies, unless it was implicitly believed that he was ultimate owner of the land.

These donations undoubtedly indicate that the king had the supreme ownership over the whole village; otherwise he could not transfer such comprehensive rights over the whole village in such a way. Moreover, in these cases the donees not only acquired the right to receive a certain amount of the royal revenue, but also, on some occasions, they enjoyed all kinds of royal dues which are always specially recorded in the inscriptions.[47] It is not stated in any inscription that they had right to dispossess peasants at will and we assume that this right was not accorded to them, though no doubt they could punish or evict tenants who refused to pay their dues.

In some cases also some portion of a village land is donated. But the nature of the grant in such instances was not the same in the case of a whole village with its varied population dwelling on all kinds of land. In any case, the peasants' tenureship of the land remained the same; and in both the types of grant, the villagers, who used to pay the revenue to the king, would henceforth, pay the same to the donee instead of the king.[48] In other words, such a grant implied the transfer of revenue from the state to the donee; and the state remained only some prerogative rights over the village. But in the case of a single field the donees enjoyed the fruit of the soil, and in most cases were exempted from payment of royal dues. Moreover, there is no record of the donation of a whole village except by the king. This leaves no reason for doubt that the king was thought of as the ultimate owner of the villages.

Even after the donation of land, the king reserved certain prerogative rights over the donated lands, such as the right of imposing fines on thieves.[49] Moreover, the new owner was not allowed to exact any new taxes from the people of the donated area, and was liable to punishment or the annulment of his rights if he imposed any new taxes. The donee, enjoying tax-free villages or lands, was forbidden to encourage revenue-paying cultivators, artisans etc. from other villages to immigrate into the donated village for this would involve loss of revenue to the state.[50] In certain land grants, the state still has specific rights of enjoyment.[51] Furthermore, certain conditions of tenureship are imposed on land grants. Thus, in the case of lands granted under the terms of *nīvī-dharma*, *akṣaya-nīvī-dharma*, *aprada-nīvī-dharma* etc., the donees have no right to alienate them by sale, mortgage etc.[52]

To purchase and donate a piece of land, ordinary citizens had to take permission from the state.[53] For this purpose, they had to apply to the state through authorities. Thus, when Vatabhoga purchased a triple *kulya vapa* of cultivated land at the rate of 4 *dīnaras* from the local bodies of the *bhukti* of Varaka, he had to take the permission from the district governor.[54] State sanction was specially required for these cases, because only the state had authority to exempt the land from all kinds of royal dues. But, it is not possible to establish whether the sanction of the state was required in ordinary secular land transactions, for we have no such sale deeds in our period.

In most of the inscriptions, it is specially stated that the king has no right to confiscate land granted by him or by his predecessors. But in some cases, the king reserves the right of confiscation under certain circumstances. In the Chammak Copper Plate of Pravarasena-II, it is stated that "this condition of the charter should be maintained by *Brahmaṇas* and by (future) lords, namely (the enjoyment of this grant belongs to *Brahmaṇas*) for the same time with the moon and the sun, provided that they commit no treason against the kingdom consisting of seven constituent parts of (successive) kings; that they are no slayers of *Brahmaṇas*, and are not thieves, adulterers, prisoners of kings etc.; that they do not wage war; (and) that they do not wrong other villagers. But, if they act otherwise, or assent (to such acts), the king will commit no theft in taking the land away."[55] We thus see that the king still has some protective rights over the donated areas of the village Charmanka. We also hear of the endowment of a field which was previously enjoyed by a merchant. The grants of Mahārāja Svāmidāsa state: "I hereby consent to the *Brahmaṇa* grant of a field, the holding of the merchant Āryya, situated in the village of south Valmikatalla-vataka in the district of Nāgarika, to the *Brāhmaṇa* named *Munda*. . ." But, it is not made clear whether the land was purchased from Āryya.[56] If it was not duly purchased, it must have been appropriated from the original owner by the royal prerogative right. According to the legal tradition, the king could appropriate the wealth and property of a dead subject who had no heir. This is supported by Bṛhaspati and Nārada who hold that if a Kṣatriya, Vaiśya or Śudra die without male issue, or wife, or brother, their property should be taken in escheat by the king, for he is the lord of all.[57] In modern times, M.H. Gopal agrees with F.W. Thomas that the king is the proprietor of land for he is entitled to revenue and could replace a defaulting cultivator from his holding. Gopal believes that it was sort of tenant under the crown.[58]

It may be noted that mines were regarded as a state monopoly. The earlier law-givers such as Viṣṇu states that everything dug up from mines belong to the king.[59] In the opinion of Manu, also the king obtains one-half of the ancient hoards and metals found in the ground, by reasons of his giving protection and because he is the lord of the soil.[60] The king had also the monopoly over the treasure trove (*nidhi*). As we see from the numerous inscriptions in which the king gave such right of enjoyment to the donees.[61] Nārada and many other earlier law-givers include treasure trove as one of the sources of the state wealth.[62]

3.5 Community Ownership

But some sources reject the idea of the king's ultimate ownership of land. In a *Jātaka* story, a king tells his mistress that he cannot give her the kingdom, for he is not its owner.[63] When a legendary king, Visva Karman Bhauvuna gave land to the priests, the goddess of earth rose up in person and rebuked to give her away.[64] A mediaeval commentator possibly basing his argument on this story, says that the kings cannot give away land for it is owned in common.

Dr. R.G. Basak upholds the concept of corporate ownership of land by the villagers.[65] He argues that if the lands belong to the state, "why could it not alternate them without the consent or approval of the people's representatives, the *Mahattaras* and other businessmen (*vyavahārins*) of the province and the district, and sometimes even the common folk? Why is that the government did not take upon itself the whole responsibility of transferring to others by sale hitherto unassessed, untilled *khas* land?" This proves that these lands belonged not to the state but to the whole village or village-assemblies, and hence, their transfer could not take place without the consent or approval of the latter. It appears that neither the state nor the village elders could sell the lands singly. In the plate of Dharmāditya-I, it is recorded that only one-sixth of the sale proceeds went to the state treasury and the rest went to the village assembly.[66] This proves the land in transaction belonged to the village community, the state received one-sixth of the produces because it sanctioned the transaction. He argues that these facts undoubtedly prove that land owned by the people themselves and not by the state, and the state could only receive taxes in return for the protection given to them.

R.C. Majumdar and A.S. Altekar support Basak. According to Majumdar, the village corporation "were practically the absolute proprietors of the village lands, including fresh clearings, and were responsible for the total amount of rent to the government. In case the owner of a plot of land failed to pay his share, it became the property of the corporation which had right to dispose of it to realize the dues."[67]

Similarly, Altekar suggests that "the ownership of the cultivable land vested in private individual or families, and not in the state."[68]

Regarding the ownership of land, Jaiminī, the famous author of the *Mīmāṁsa-sūtra*, holds that in the *Visvajit* sacrifice, where the sacrificer has to donate everything that belongs to him, even an emperor cannot make a gift of the whole land of which may be the ruler, for the earth is common to all.[69] Śabara Svāmin, the commentators of the *Mīmāṁsa-sūtra* elaborates this by adding that others have as much right over the earth as the emperor.[70] The emperor is entitled to a share of crops produced from the earth, for he protects them. But, all other persons also walk on the earth; produce crops on it and get their substance from it, and so they also have rights over the earth. Therefore, there is no difference between the emperor and other persons as to rights over the earth.[71]

The same view is held by modern European scholars like J.S. Hegel, Maine and Haden-Powell.[72] They hold in general that the people in India regarded the land not as their personal property but as the property of the community. Each individual merely possessed his land by virtue of his descent from an ancestor who was the founder of the village; the village land belonged to the village as a whole. In recent times Indian scholars like D.D. Kośāmbi and R.S. Sharma developed the concept of Indian feudalism. According to Kośāmbi, the first feudal period consisting of a closed peasant economy of early Christian era constituted feudalism from above and afterwards kings made land-grants to subordinates which gave rise to a feudalism from below as in the form of a class of landlords that developed within the village.[73]

3.6 Private Ownership

Dr. K.P. Jayaswal holds the theory of ultimate private ownership of land in ancient India.[74] The *Jātakas* record the donation of land for park by Jivaka at Rājagriha and by Ambapāli at Vaiśali and Anantapindaka at Śravasti. The judicial verdict in respect of Anantapindaka suit against Jeta proves individual ownership of land with the right of transfer by sale.[75] But, theory of Jayaswal has been refuted by Dr. U.G. Ghosal and Dr. A.L. Basham.[76] Ghosal argues: "Three out of the texts quoted by Jayaswal to disprove the king's ownership of the land do not support his case, but prove that just the contrary." On the other hand, the evidence of Minmā text (VI 7.3) which Dr. Jayaswal in the same context quotes, along with the commentaries thereon, is no less decisive as to the denial of the king's proprietary right. Same is the view of A.L. Basham.[77]

3.7 Intermediaries between the State and the People

Be that as it may, we find from the Maurya period, may even before that, the royal ownership concept began to gain ground and the kings of ancient India did have a hierarchy of vassals and officials, land-holders, village headmen or donees to whom administrative, judicial and revenue powers were conferred. The vanquished princes, when defeated in the battle or accepted the overlordship of a paramount power, become a tributary to the latter and were discharged administrative, judicial and revenue functions independently; such a vassal was supposed to assist his overlord with troops and fund in war. This is supported by the epics and the *Smṛti* literature, of course, the policy was not uniformly followed. These vassals had vassals of their own or local chieftains who were styled as *Rājanas*, *Sāmantas*, *Mahasāmantas*, *Bhojas* etc.

Again sometimes the king paid their officers and favourites not by cash but with their right to collect revenues from a village or a group of villages. The Maurya paid many officers by granting them lands; the *Sāmantas* referred in the *Arthaśāstra* is a pointer to that. Harṣa kept one-fourth of his crown land for public servants. The practice might have been continued between the Maurya and Gupta period. The Pālas and Pratihāras also rewarded their vassals and officers by granting revenue of villages. The practice is confirmed by Hiuen-tsang and Kalhana's *Rājtarangini*, in Kaśmir. In the south, such practice is confirmed by Chola temple inscriptions and the service tenure of the vassals of the Vijayanagara empire.

The Nānāghāt cave inscription of Naganikā (1st century B.C.), the Nāsik cave inscription and Kārla Buddhist cave inscription of Usāvadatta (2nd century), the Nāsik and Kārla cave inscription of Gautamiputra Satakarni and Vasisthputra Śri Pulumai (2nd century), the Hatigumpha inscriptions of Khāravela chief Queen in Orissa and the Maidavolu inscription of Siṁhavarman (3rd century) confirm the Buddhist and Jain monasteries as well as the Hindu temples held considerable estates.

These estates carried with them other privileges of executive and judicial nature. These recipients became intermediaries between the king and the people giving birth to so called feudalism and above.

Yet there was another factor which gave birth to hereditary land and estate holders. The Āryans, when took to the agricultural settlements over which a clan or a tribe undertook collective cultivation as some Greek authors like Strabo and Diodoras held. The land was held in common and each family was allocated a portion of the village land. The affairs of the village for revenue, justice, law and order were administered by the village elders in village assemblies. But their duties tended gradually to be performed by able persons and office bearers for different works were appointed. These able personalities gave birth to the hereditary village administrators termed as *Gramiṇi, Kulaputras* etc. were looked upon as king's representative to be replaced at his pleasure. They controlled and administered justice, police and revenue deposits. Some privileges in the form of land grants were given to them. This is what termed as feudalism from below.

Now, we have to remember that the term feudalism is coined in European perspective, and is closely connected with the monarchic system. In Europe the kingdom of the different princes were divided into fiefs over which a military chief was placed on contractual basis. The lord was under obligation to provide a fixed number of soldiers as and when demanded by his prince. The lord or the military chief subdivided his territory to his retinues who were under his control and subjection and were under obligation to serve in the Army. Thus, in Europe contractual relation covered the whole society from the king to the villain.

But in India, the conditions were different. The essential features of European feudalism as mode of production and distribution is absent in Indian scenario. In the Indian fiefs, the chief might be in some cases held on condition of supplying troop to the overlord, but the people of his domain were under no obligation to go for military service. The lords collected revenue stipulated and even exacted forced labour, dispensed justice and police duties in their respective areas but could not ask for military service compulsorily from the people. Moreover, there was no restriction on the mobility of the people in estates held by such landlords. Hence, a fundamental different condition existed in India. It is possibly unfair to generalize it as feudalism. In the absence of a generally accepted parlance, it may be called quasi-feudalism of India.

3.8 Land Tenure

Our knowledge of agrarian relations in ancient India is extremely vague and poor. The land grants for religious purposes refer to some terms which provide some idea about land relations. These terms are: (i) *nīvī-dharma*, (ii) *akṣaya-nīvī-dharma* or *akṣaya-nīvī*, (iii) *nīvī-dharma-akṣaya*, (iv) *paradā-dharma*, (v) *aparadakṣaya-nīvī-dharma* or *aparadakṣaya-nīvī-maryādā*, and (v) *bhūmichhidranyaya.*[78]

The expressions *nīvī* and *nīvī-dharma* have been interpreted by Indologists in different ways. Jayaswal says *nīvī* is a technical term which means a dispatch document, record or file (*Āyavyaya-nīvī*;

Āyavyaya-viśuddha-nīvī; *Samudrapustabhānda-nīvī kānāmekatra*; *Āyavyaya-nīvī-nāmagrāni*.[79] The expression, like our modern 'red tape' is derived from physical feature of the string which ties round the dispatch or returns. The *nīvī* of the inscription has, thus, to be interpreted as document or dispatch and *Akṣaya-nīvī* as permanent document.[80]

R.G. Basak has refused Jayaswal's contention.[81] He holds Jayaswal probably kept in view the meaning of *vastra-bandhanam*, as offered to this word by lexicographers, when he proposes that the word *nīvī* of the inscriptions is to be interpreted as document or dispatch and *akṣaya-nīvī* as permanent document. Basak points out that the most important meaning of the word *nīvī*, as given in the *Amarakoṣa* and by Hemachandra which would well suit the passages in the inscriptions and the *Arthaśāstra*, has escaped the notice of Jayaswal. In the *Amarkoṣa* we find that the word *nīvī* has been used as synonymous with *paripāna* or *mūldhana* (*i.e.*, the capital or principal) in sale and purchase and such other transactions.[82] Similarly, Hemachandra puts *mulyadravya* as synonym for *nīvī*.[83] It may be seen that whenever the word *nīvī* has been used in Indian inscriptions it is to be explained as fixed capital out of interest (*vṛddi*) on which a particular expense is to be met. Hence, to make a gift of land or money according to *nīvī-dharma* is to give it on condition that the endowment is to be maintained perpetual. The donee can only spend the interest for the specified purpose. The interpretation is also corroborated by the evidence of Damodarpur Copper Plate, where it is stated that the land should be enjoyed as long as the moon, the sun and stars exist.[84]

The passage from the *Arthaśāstra* referred by Jayaswal can be cited in refutation of the *nīvī*, as suggested by him. It here means that which remains as the net balance after consideration of all receipts (*āya*) and payment (*vyaya*). Again the term in another passage in the same *Arthaśāstra* prescribes the various forms of punishment for scraping off, eating up and destroying the *nīvī*. A document certainly cannot be eaten up. That *nīvī* cannot mean dispatch, can also be shown by reference to another passage in the *Arthaśāstra* where we read of the bringing together or verification of receipts (*āyam samānayet*) and of expenditure (*vyayam samānayet*).[85]

Thus taking all the above facts in consideration, it appears that an endowment of this type was to be maintained perpetual by the donee but that he could make use of the income accruing from it. Its implication will be further clear when we consider the other fiscal terms such as *akṣaya-nīvī-dharma*, *apradakṣaya-nīvī-dharma*, *aparadakṣaya-nīvī-maryādā*, *nīvī-dharmākṣaya*.

Sometimes, the word *akṣaya* is added to *nīvī* in order to give more emphasis to the permanency of the endowment, for the word *akṣaya* literally means indestructible or perpetual. This can better be taken as an extension of the meaning of *nīvī-dharma*. The lands or money endowed according to this principle were to be treated as *akṣaya-nīvī*, where the original endowment was in no circumstances to be destroyed or diminished.[86] This is further indicated by the fact that where the word *akṣaya-nīvī-dharma* is mentioned, in some cases we have also the expression *svātachandra-taraka* as in the Pāhārpur and the Baigrām copper plates.[87] It thus indicates that the endowment was perpetual and could be possessed, theoretically, as long as the sun, the moon and the stars exist.

We find references of this kind of tenureship from earlier and later inscriptions also. In the Nāsik cave inscription, we find that *Uṣavadāta* granted 3000 *karṣapānas* as perpetual endowment (*akṣaya-nīvī-kāhapāna-sahasrāni trīni*) which were invested in two parts of 2000 and 1000 *karṣapānas* each in two weaver guilds. It is explicitly mentioned there that these *karṣapānas* were not to be repaid (*apadāditāva*) but their interest only was to be enjoyed (*vadhi-bhojā*).[88] In the passage in the Sānchi stone inscription of A.D. 450-451, it is also found that Upāsaka Harisvāminī made a grant of 12 *dīnaras* as *akṣaya-nīvī* to the *saṁgha* in the great monastery of Kakonadabhota *akṣaya-nīvī dāttā dināra dvadāsa*.[89] There also it is clearly pointed out that a *bhikṣu* is to be fed daily out of the interest that accrues from this endowment (*esām dināranam ya vṛddhirupajāyate tayā divase divase samgha madhya-pravistaka-bhikṣu-ekam bhojayitavyah*). Again in a passage of the Bihar inscription of Skandagupta we read of the grant of a village field (*grāmakṣetra* as an *akṣaya-nīvī* or a permanent endowment).[90]

In certain cases, as in the case of Dhanaidaha copper plate of Kumārgupta-I, the above terms of tenureship is reversed. It is here stated that a place named Kṣudraka was in possession of Śiva Śarma and Nāgaśarma which afterwards was donated to Varāhasvāmin after reversing the process of *nīvī-dharma*.[91] The new owner acquired the full right to enjoy the endowment with the power of transfer and sale. Here the term *kṣaya* is (*nīvīdharma-kṣaya*) implies the destruction of the principle of *nīvī dharma*. U.N. Ghosal interprets the term in different way and suggests the reading of *nīvīdharma-kṣayana* or *nīvīdharma-akṣayana*. He then translates it as "according to the custom of non-destruction of *nīvīdharma*".[92] But the Dhanaidaha copper plate inscription seems to contradict this explanation. It quite clearly suggests that the principle of *nīvī-dharma* was reversed and the intending purchaser wanted to buy land by destroying the condition of non-transferability of it, that is, to buy it with the future right of alienation.

Another term is *apradādharma*, *apradā* literally means *na-pradā*, *i.e.* that which cannot be alienated or which does not yield anything.[93] Thus the grant of land, according to Apradāsharma, perhaps means the donee has all the rights to enjoy such property but has no right to further gift the same and can only enjoy the interest and income that accrue from the endowed land. In other words, just like *nīvī-dharma*, the original endowment must not be diminished or destroyed, but must be preserved intact to perpetuity. We thus see that one Amartadeva endowed fine *kulyavāpas* of *khila* land with *vāstu*, according to the Apradādharma, to *Bhagavan Svetavaraha-Svāmin* (*i.e.* the God Viṣṇu).[94]

Therefore, *nīvī*, *akṣaya-nīvīdharma* and *apradādharma* indicate almost the same kind of tenureship of land. The term *apradākṣayanīvī* occurs in Damodarpur copper plate of Kumārgupta of A.D. 448-449.[95] Basak holds: "It seems doubtful whether this applicant wanted the land on the nullification or continuation of the condition of non-transferability, the word *apradākṣaya* admitting of an interpretation applicable both ways."[96] However, the interpretation of Ghoshal seems to be more suitable. As with *nīvī-dharma*, the donee has the full right of perpetual enjoyment of the endowment, but has no power to alienate or destroy or diminish it.[97]

Another important fiscal term we come across is *bhūmicchidranyāya*. It occurs in the inscription of the Khoh copper plate of Sarbanātha, the Māliya copper plate of Dharmasena, the Alina copper plate of Śilāditya-VII and many others in the later period. There is a great deal of controversy among scholars on the interpretation of this technical term.

Dr. R.G. Bhandarkar is of the opinion that *bhūmicchidranyāya* may have some reference to the circumstances where the holes in the earth are not permanent, but are filled up in course of time. In the context he relates a story from the *Taitiriya Saṁhita* (11.5) and from *Bhāgavata* (VI.9). Indra killed Vivarupa, the son of Tvastr and then transferred his sin to the earth. But in consideration of her having taken in, he gave her a boon, by which all holes made in her would be filled up in time. The sense of the sentence then is that a grant is to last as long as the moon, the sun etc. exist. As holes of the earth are filled up in time and the earth is whole again and so unchanged, so a grant should survive revolutions and last unchanged for ever.[98]

Bühler supports the explanation of Bhandarkar. The *bhūmicchidra* is the "reasoning from the familiar instance of the ground and cleft, or clefts therein, or the inference that the whole includes the parts, just as a piece of land includes the various clefts therein. If it is stated in this and other grants that a village or like is given *bhūmicchidranyāya*, it means simply that it is made over with all its appurtenances, produce, right etc."[99]

Barnett follows the rendering of Yādavaprakāśa and Kauṭilya. He believes that *bhūmicchidranyāya* would naturally mean the same condition as that under which tenants hold land in wilderness, forests etc., *i.e.* precario, with reservation of the king's right to eject them at will."[100] But Ghoshal extends the meaning of it a little further and in his opinion the term "implies the grant of full right of ownership, such as would be acquired by a person making fallow land cultivable for the first time."[101]

Bhandarkar more or less follows Barnett. *Bhūmicchidranyāya* literally means "according to the principle of a whole in the earth". In his opinion this term occur in some such phrases as *purvapratha devabrahmadeya varijjitah bhūmicchidranyāyaenandrarkkarnnavakṣittisar parvatasamakalersah putra-poutra-nyayabhogya udakaisarggena dharmadaya nisrstah yatah*[102] in the inscriptions, though sometimes without it, and it is to be connected grammartically with the word "*nisrstah*" that follows. It appears from this that these terms signify the reservation from the gift. The word seems to reserve the right of guarantor to the mineral resources and treasure-trove etc. The right of the king to these is always urged against a gift unless it is expressly transferred. The word, therefore, may reserve this right in favour of the royal donor in spite of the gift of the land.

If we go carefully through these records, we see that most of the lands granted under this rule are cultivable lands. In some cases, a whole village is granted under this tenureship and a village must include all kinds of lands. In the earlier period, this term may have indicated land unfit for cultivation, as we find in Kauṭilya and it may have retained this meaning in some circles, as it is attested to Yādavaprakāśa. But from the sources of the Gupta period, it is quite impossible to agree with those who give the term this interpretation. Moreover, as regards its implications for the system of land tenure, *bhūmicchidranyāya* very clearly indicates permanent land ṭenureship, and the property endowed under this rule is freely handed down from generation to generation.

From the above analysis, it can also be said that tenureship like *nīvīdharma* was prevalent in many parts of northern India at least from the time of the Guptas onwards. But, the five other kinds of tenureship of land were probably mainly followed in the eastern part of the Gupta empire, because they are very frequently mentioned in the inscriptions from Bengal.

3.9 Land Survey and Measurement

The complex land system and an elaborate revenue required proper survey and measurement. Pāṇini refers to the officers *Kṣetrakara* who divided the cultivable lands into plots by survey and measurement and fixed their area.[103] The *Jātaka* stories refer to local officers as "holder of surveyor's) card, the *rajjugahaka*. The officers mentioned in the Aśkan inscriptions as *rajjuka* may have been the same.[104] Megasthenes records that the land was surveyed and proper record was maintained. Land transfer to a new owner could take place after reference to the local land records. Boundaries and locations of villages were clearly marked and defined and we learn from the Junnār Buddhist cave inscriptions[105] that the donated field was delimited. Such demarcations and delimitations are indicated in a large number of inscriptions. Village boundaries were indicated by river, mountain, forest, cave, artificial buildings, temples, trees etc. and rules framed by law-givers were fairly applied. The various marks facilitated the survey work. Violations of boundaries or marks were severely dealt with Kauṭilya and Manu[106] prescribed fines. Penalties for violation of boundary marks are also prescribed in the *Viṣṇusmṛti*, *Yājñavalkyasmṛti* and the *Mahābhārata*.[107] The land sale or transfer deeds recorded the name of the record-keeper who certified its transferability.[108]

We do not have any definite idea about the land survey and measurement operations. Survey were undertaken by means of measuring rod (*daṇdaka*) to which a rope was tied to assist in the measurement of land. The surveyors (*Rajjugahaka-amacca*) must have encountered difficulties in carrying on their duties. Pāṇini *kṣetrakara* demarcated cultivable areas into fields by actual survey and measurement. In the *Jātakas*, we come across the linear measures like *karisa* and *rajju*.[109] Kauṭilya mentions a list of the following measures, *viz. karisa, angula, daṇda, aratni, dhanus, goruta* etc. He also sometimes mentions *paridesa, bahu, ditasti, chhāyapuruṣa, yojana* as measures.[110]

Rajju, daṇda and *nivartana* continued to be current even after Kauṭilya. Other known units are *pada* (*padavarta*), *kulavapya, nana* (*nalika*) etc.[111] According to Kauṭilya, one *nivartana* was equal to three *rajjus*.[112] The linear measurement became current in the north as well as in the south. It was also current among the western Chalukyas, but another linear measure is known from the western Chalukyas' records as *rajamanas*, the exact length of which cannot be made out.[113] *Nivartana* was also in vogue under the Kadambas and Raṣtrakūtas and also in Bihar till recently[114] (known in local dialect as *netana*). The length and breadth of a *nivartana* varied with time and locality.

Mattar was also current under the western Chalukyas. *Padavarta* was used in Gujarāt and Saurāṣtra.[115] *Bhūmi* was another measure in measuring land and the word has been utilized in the *Satpatha Brahmaṇa* and is also mentioned in the inscription of Pravarsena-II.[116] *Nala* of the epigraph was no other than the abbreviated form of *nalika* of Kauṭilya.[117] It is also mentioned in *Panchatantra*, the *Bhagavata* and Damodarpur copper plate and also in Barrakpur grant of Vijaysena.[118] *Hasta* was another form of measurement and is mentioned by Kauṭilya.[119] The Junagarh inscription of Rudradamana (A.D. 150-152) and in various other Bengal grants, *kulyavāpa*, *droṇavāpa*, *ardhavāpa* are mentioned as units of measurement.[120] Kālidāsa has used this system as simile in describing Raghu's conquest of Vanas. According to Hoernle, one it implied so much of land as is usually with a *kulya* of seed. *Kulyavāpa* may mean an area of land one which one *kulya* of seed could be grown.[121] *Hala* was another unit. It is explained as area cultivated by one *hala* and the multiples of *hala* (plough). In one of the Prakrit inscriptions, hundred of thousands of ploughs of land were granted. A similar account is found in the Pallava record.

According to Danamayukha, a donor should give a *grāma* to *Brāhmaṇa* but if he is not in a position to do this he may give land measuring a *gocharaṇa*.[122] This area of land may be equal to whereupon a hundred cows and an ox can sit easily, *i.e.* the produce of which is sufficient to support a *Brahmaṇa* for a year.[123] Baudhayan holds that a portion of land is necessary to support a family.[124] Large varieties of measures were in vogue in ancient India and some of them differed from state to state. States, in different parts, might have some different measures.

REFERENCES

1. *Amarkoṣa* 1.5, pp. 6, 10-13, and 70-72.
2. *Epigraphia Indica*, Pt. A, p. 195, Pt. B, p. 200.
3. S.K. Maity, *Economic Life of Northern India in the Gupta Period*, p. 33.
4. *Amarkoṣa* 1.5, p. 70.

5. S.K. Maity, *Economic Life of Northern India in the Gupta Period*, p. 34.
6-10. *Ibid.*
11. *Nārada*, X, p. 26.
12-14. S.K. Maity, *Economic Life of Northern India in the Gupta Period*, p. 35.
15-17. *Ibid.*
18-22. *Ibid.*, p. 36.
23. S.K. Maity, *Economic Life of Northern India in the Gupta Period*, p. 24.
24. *Manu*, IX, p. 4.
25-26. R. Chowdhury, *An Economic History of Ancient India*, p. 49.
27. Vinegradoff's *Jurisprudence*, pp. 324-51.
28. *Jajna*, ii, p. 446.
29. *Bṛhaspati*, VII, pp. 24-25.
30. *Nārada*, I, pp. 84-87.
31. *Ibid.*
32. *Ibid.*
33. *Ibid.*
34. *Gautama*, II, p. 4.
35. *Manu*, X, p. 115.
36. *Bṛhaspati*, VII, p. 23.
37. *Nārada*, I, p. 51.
38. *Gautama*, VIII, p. 39.
39. R. Chowdhury, *op. cit.*, p. 50.
40. *Manu*, VIII, p. 39.
41. *Gautama*, IX, p. 1.
42. *Bṛhaspati*, XVI, p. 119.
43. R. Chowdhury, *op. cit.*, p. 51.
44. *Ibid.*
45. McCrindle, *Ancient India as described by Megasthenes and Arrian*, pp. 42-43.
46. S.K. Maity, *Economic Life of Northern India in the Gupta Period*, pp. 24-25.
47. *Ibid.*
48. *Ibid.*, p. 25.
49. *Ibid.*, p. 26.
50. *Ibid.*, pp. 26-27.
51. *Ibid.*
52. *Ibid.*
53. *Ibid.*
54. *Ibid.*
55. *Ibid.*
56. *Ibid.*
57. *Ibid.*
58. R. Chowdhury, *op. cit.*, p. 55.
59. *Viṣṇu*, III, p. 55.
60. *Manu*, VIII, p. 39.
61. S.K. Maity, *op. cit.*, p. 29.
62. *Nārada*, VII, p. 7.
63. *Jātaka*, VI 7, p. 3.
64. S.K. Maity, *op. cit.*, p. 32.
65. *Ibid.*, pp. 29-30.
66. *Ibid.*
67. *Ibid.*

68. *The Vakataka Gupta Age*, p. 333.
69. S.K. Maity, *op. cit.*, pp. 31-32.
70. *Ibid.*
71. *Ibid.*
72. Ronald Enden, *Imaging India*, Oxford (paperback), 1992.
73. *Ibid.*
74. K.P. Jayaswal, *The Hindu Policy*, p. 343.
75. R. Chowdhury, *op. cit.*, p. 49.
76. S.K. Maity, *op. cit.*, p. 32.
77. *Ibid.*
78. S.K. Maity, *op. cit.*, pp. 36-37.
79. *Ibid.*
80. *Ibid.*
81. *Ibid.*
82. *Amarakoṣa*, pp. 9, 80, 218.
83. S.K. Maity, *op. cit.*, p. 38.
84. *Epigraphia Indica*, XV, p. 130.
85. *Arthaśāstra*, ii, pp. 7, 64.
86. S.K. Maity, *op. cit.*, p. 38.
87. *Ibid.*
88. *Epigraphia Indica*, VIII, p. 82.
89. *Ibid.*, 'e'.
90. *Ibid.*, 'b'.
91. *Epigraphia Indica*, XVII, p. 347.
92. *H.R.S.*, p. 199.
93. *Epigraphia Indica*, V, p. 143.
94. *Ibid.*
95. *Epigraphia Indica*, XV, p. 133.
96. *A.M.S.J.*, III, Part 2, p. 481.
97. *H.R.S.*, p. 199.
98. *I.A.*, 1872, Vol. 1, p. 46.
99. *I.A.*, 1875, p. 106.
100. S.K. Maity, *Economic Life of Northern India in the Gupta Period*, pp. 43-44.
101. *Ibid.*
102. *Epigraphia Indica*, XI, p. 177.
103. R. Chowdhury, *op. cit.*, p. 66.
104. A.L. Basham, *op. cit.*, p. 109.
105. R. Chowdhury, *op. cit.*, p. 67.
106. *Ibid.*
107. *Ibid.*
108. S.K. Maity, *op. cit.*, p. 67.
109. R. Chowdhury, *op. cit.*, p. 67.
110. *Ibid.*
111. *Ibid.*
112. *Ibid.*
113. *Ibid.*
114. *Epigraphia Indica*, X, pp. 102-06, XI, p. 280.
115. R. Chowdhury, *op. cit.*, p. 68.

116-118. *Ibid.*

119. S.K. Maity, *Economic Life of Northern India in the Gupta Period*, p. 49.
120. *Ibid.*, p. 52.
121. *Ibid.*, pp. 53-60.
122. *Epigraphia Indica*, XX, p. 18.
123. R. Chowdhury, *op. cit.*, p. 68.
124. *Ibid.*, p. 69.

4

AGRICULTURE, GARDENING AND CATTLE-FARMING

Agriculture is the main stay of Indian economy even today. The chief productive occupation of the *Vedic Aryans* was also agriculture and cattle-breeding. The various stages of agriculture such as ploughing, sowing in burrows, cutting of corn and making bundles of sheaves and thrashing and winnowing are referred in the *Vedas* and rituals were prescribed for some of them.[1] Prayers for success in agriculture are not infrequent. At the time of the Mauryas, Vārta, which included agriculture, cattle-breeding and dairy farming, trade and commerce had become so important that the king was advised to study Vārta carefully.[2] Though these were the professions of *Vaiśyas* and secondary profession of the *Śūdras*, the *Brāhamaṇas* and the *Kṣatriyas* were allowed to pursue these in times of emergency as *āpada dharma*.[3] According to the Greek writers, the most of the people in India lived upon grains and agriculture was the basis of the economic life of the Gupta age.[4] Fa-hien states that agriculture was the principal industry of the villages.[5] Tamils in the early period regarded it as one of the learned arts.[6] Even ascetics cultivated land for their maintenance.[7]

Development of land was the principal factor in success of agriculture. The state and the community were enjoined to strive for the prosperity of agriculture. The creation of beneficial interest by law in favour of the person who first cleared the forest or reclaimed waste land, facilitated the clearing of jungles and bringing of waste land under cultivation. In the interest of agriculture, the non-cultivating proprietors were discouraged.[8] Milindapānho and Manu favoured the idea that those who cleared the forest and prepared fields for cultivation, would be granted ownership of the lands.[9] Śukra laid down certain benevolent rules for reclaiming waste land; if the people undertake cultivating waste land, digging tanks, canals, wells etc. for their improvement, the king should not demand anything from them, until they realize profit amounting to twice their expenditure.[10] For the encouragement of agriculture, the king granted quite large areas of cultivable land. The Buddhist and Jain *Saṁghas* also encouraged cultivation of wastelands.[11]

The agriculturists are advised to fence their cultivated fields. Regarding fencing, Nārada provides that if the field faces a road, the fence shall be so made that a camel cannot see over it or a horse or cattle cannot jump over it and a boar cannot break through it.[12] But, if grain is destroyed by cows or other cattle crossing a fence, the herdsman should be punished unless he tries his best to keep the cattle off.[13] When grain is destroyed together with root, the owner of it may claim a corresponding quantity of grain as damage, the herdsman is to be punished corporeally; and a fine should be imposed on his master.[14] In case the mischief is done by a cow or a female buffalo, the king shall inflict a fine of one *māsa* or two *māsa* respectively; but in case it is done by a goat or a sheep trespassing with its young, the fine shall be half a *māsa*.[15] Impunity is granted to cows recently calved or unmanageable. When cows trespass because of the fault of herdsman, the owner shall not be punished, only the herdsman is liable to punishment.[16] But, when the herdsman is seized by the king or devoured by an alligator, or struck by or bitten by serpent, or has fallen from a tree or is killed by ferocious animals or becomes the victim of a disease, neither the herdsman nor the owner of the cattle shall be punished.[17] Impunity is granted to the herdsmen if a field is situated on the borders of the village or contiguous to a pasture ground, or adjacent to high road or if the field is not well fenced.[18]

Intrusion of actors, dancers, signers, drummers, buffoons and wandering minstrels were banned from the village in the interest of agriculture.[19] The king and his officers were advised to remain outside the village.[20] Soldiers were allowed to enter the village only on official business but not to have any deal with villagers.[21] The villagers were allowed the facility of uninterrupted cultivation, says Megasthenes.[22] The cultivators were guaranteed fair price and any attempt of businessmen or community to exploit them were prevented.[23] They were exempted from arrest for non-payment of debt. During the cultivating season, loans were repayable in easy installments and remissions were granted for the importation of new and rare seeds.[24]

In consideration of importance of agriculture, stealing of grains and other products of the soil and agricultural implements were dealt with. Nārada lays down that destroying, disfiguring or otherwise injuring fruits, roots, water courses and the like or agricultural implements is a

Ṣahasa of the first kind and the punishment should be proportionate to the magnitude of the crime but should not be less than a hundred *pānas*.[25] Bṛhaspati lays down that the stealer of the grain shall be compelled to give ten times as much to the owner and a double amount as fine.[26] He who steals more than ten *kumbhas* of grain should be put to death; but, if the man steals less than that, he should be compelled to restore the stolen grain to the owner and a fine of eleven times the quantity should be imposed.[27] He further provides that if a man destroys or takes away implements of husbandry or damages an embankment, flowers, roots or fruits, he shall be fined a hundred *pānas* or more according to the nature of the offence.[28] When a man takes away grain, wood, flowers or fruits without permission, he deserves a hand to be cut off.[29]

4.1 Agricultural Process

Pāṇini and the Buddhist sources describe the agricultural process in detail. So also Milindapānho provides information of ploughing, sowing, irrigation, fencing, watching, reaping, thrashing and also of storage of granary.[30] Lands were carefully prepared for sowing. A good cultivator would cultivate his land twice or thrice before sowing. Then good seeds were sown.[31] A spade or hoe was used for loosening the soil for the encouragement of the seedlings. When corn was ripe, sickles were used to reap it.[32] It was then gathered on the thrashing floor and after thrashing, it was winnowed and grains were taken to granary.[33]

Oxen-driven plough was used for cultivation. *Amarkoṣa* provides a description of the plough. It consisted of the pole or shaft of the yoke, the pin of the yoke, the plough share and the tie of the yoke.[34] Bṛhaspati lays down the plough-share of iron weighing twelve *palas* should be used and it should be eight *aṅgulas* long and four *aṅgulas* broad[35] or approximately 6" by 3". But Cosmas writes that Indians use horn of the rhinoceros as plough-share. Such an information is not supported by any other source.[36]

Nearchus states that cultivation was undertaken but the whole *kinship* working in association. Each individual took as much as was calculated to support him for the year. The remainder was destroyed.[37] That might have been the case in the early stage of agricultural economy. But later from the time of the Mauryas onwards, agricultural holding became smaller and the individual peasant cultivated his land himself together with his family members; large holdings of wealthier persons were cultivated either by hired labourers or by the share-croppers.[38] Buddhist *saṁghas* gave land to the share-croppers and provided them seeds and bulls and took one-sixth of the produce.[39] Bṛhaspati, of course, provides that a man may undertake cultivation jointly with those who are his equals in point of cattle, workmen, seeds, and the like or as well as in their implements or husbandry.[40]

Greek writers say that India has a double rainfall and Indians usually gather two harvests. Eratsthones says: "India is watered by summer rains, and the plains are overflooded. During these rains, accordingly, flax, miller, and also sesamum, rice and bosmura are sown, and in the winter rice, wheat, barley, pulse and other esculent fruits unknown to us are sown."[41] But in *Bṛhatsaṁhita* we have reference to summer crops, winter crops, and autumn crops. Therefore, three crops were grown in the later period of ancient India.[42]

Bṛhaspati has given salutary advise to cultivators. He says that cultivators should refrain from cultivating an enclosed pasture-ground, land adjacent to a town, or a king's highway, barren soil and ground infected by mice.[43] On the other hand, he who cultivates the land which is fertile, has many holes, is wet, is capable of irrigation, is surrounded by fields on all sides, in due season will profit much.[44] Moreover, sensible cultivators should not use cattle which are lean, very old, small, diseased, apt to run away, blind, one-eyed or lame for ploughing.[45]

4.2 Agricultural Products

The agricultural products may be classified as under:

> (i) Cereals, (ii) pulses, (iii) oil-seeds, (iv) fibres, (v) dyes, (vi) drugs, (vii) spices, (viii) vegetables, (ix) fruits, (x) pot-herbs, and (xi) fodder.[46]

This division, however, is not very logical as some products may belong to different categories.

Rice was grown on the fields which received heavy rainfall. Gangetic valley, Andhra, Tamil Nadu, Bengal, Assam and Orissa produced rice of several varieties.[47] Patanjali praises the *Sāli* rice of Magadha.[48] Suśruta refers to *mahā-sāli* which is also mentioned by Hiuen-tsang who was entertained with it.[49] Pāṇini mentions *byana, shastika, nivara* varieties of rice.[50] Wheat is winter-crop and was cultivated in areas of small rain-fall and must have been cultivated on the Indo-Gangetic valleys and irrigation was resorted to.[51] *Amarkoṣa* classified fields fit for cultivation of different crops like rice, wheat, barley, sesamum and pulses.[52] Besides the varieties of rice and wheat, the other food crops were barley, pea, lentil, beans and pulses of different varieties.[53] *Amarkoṣa* provides that cucumber, betel, betel-leaves, onion, garlic, pumpkin and gourd were cultivated.[54] Cultivation of sugarcane and reference to raw sugar was also given.[55]

Among the fibrous crops, principal products were cotton and flax; hemp was also not unknown.[56] Cotton was grown in Saurāṣtra and possibly in the Deccan and Tamil Nadu. Soft vegetable fibres, such as silk, cotton and black silk-cotton were also known.[57]

India grew much edible spices, oil-seeds, medicinal herbs etc. Mention may be made of mustard seeds, sesamum, linseed, lodhra, red lodhra, tamarind, ingudi, pryangu, black mustard, aloe, indigo, long pepper, pepper, cardamom, spikenard, fragrant grass, betel nuts, cloves, large cardamom, small cardamom, ginger, turmeric and saffron.[58] Southern part of India is mentioned by Kālīdāsa as the home of pepper and cardamom. Cosmos calls this part of India as the pepper country.[59]

Forests and gardens produced a large variety of fruits such as mango, palmyra, palm-fruit, orange, jack-fruit, pomegranate, grapes, bananas, coconuts and wild dates.[60]

Fodder or grass was grown to feed the domestic animals, specially the cattle. It was grown mostly in wilderness.[61]

4.3 Gardening

Bṛhatsaṁhitā provides guidance for the plantation of trees. First the gardener should sow sesamum on soft soil which should be reaped when in bloom.[62] Then the planter, duly purified, should pay honour to the tree with washing and unguents and then plant in the garden or by the house. Auspicious trees, bread-fruit, plantain, rose-apple, pomegranate and grapes are trees that, on being smeared with cow-dung, should be planted by slips or carefully grafted on the root-stump or stem of a different tree.[63] Young trees having no branches must be transplanted in the dewy season, and those that have developed branches in the winter and those with larger stems, in the rainy season. Care must be taken that they are stationed in the particular direction suiting them properly.[64] Trees before transplantation should be smeared all over the stem down to the root with ghee, oil, wax, milk and cow-dung.[65] When the trees are transplanted, they should be watered in morning and evening during summer, during the day in the cold season, and whenever the soil is dry in the rainy season.[66] Trees thus set will show the same foliage as it had before.

Trees are to be planted with enough space between them for healthy and luxuriant growth. The largest space to be left between two trees are twenty cubit or thirty feet, the middling are sixteen cubit or twenty four feet and the smallest is twelve cubit or eighteen feet, says Varāhamihira.[67] Khana in later time recommends that coconut should be planted at a distance of twelve cubits and betel-nut plants should be planted eight cubit apart.[68] Tree growing close touch each other and their roots get interwoven which kinders healthy growth and do not bear fruit properly.[69] Rose-apple, fig, grapes, pomegranate, bread-fruit etc. require moist ground, says Varāhamihira.[70]

Sometimes trees develop diseases. To heal these diseases, the cultivators are advised to trim the tree first and then to smear there ghee and mud and sprinkle them with milk and water.[71] If a tree does not bear fruit, it should be sprinkled with milk mixed with powdered peas, beans, sesamum and barley.[72] To promote the growth of fruit and blossoming of trees, creepers, shrubs and plants, the cultivators are advised to sprinkle them with a mixture of two *adhakas* of dung from sheep or goat, one *adhaka* of sesamum seeds, one *prastha* of flower, one *droṇa* of water and one *tulā* of cow-flesh; the mixture is to be infused for a week.[73]

Before planting seeds, Varāhamihira says some steps are to be taken for proper growth of plants out of them.[74] The planter should first grease his hand with ghee and then steep the seeds in milk and the seeds should be repeatedly rubbed with cow-dung mixed with flesh of bear and deer, and then seeds should be placed in a mixture of suet of hog and fish-bladder and then they are planted after ten days on the ground already prepared. The place then should be sprinkled with milk and water. Tamarind produces a sprout when sprinkled with a compound of ground rice, peas, sesamum, flour and stale-flesh; and afterwards, repeatedly mixed with turmeric. For making the wood-apple seed shoot, a powder made from the roots of various trees was recommended.

For planting a tree, Varāhamihira mentions[75] some steps to be taken. He says that a pit one cubit in diameter and twice as deep should be dug and then filled with water. Then the pit should be allowed to dry thoroughly and then that should be smeared with honey and ghee mixed with ashes. Then the pit should be filled up with ground peas, sesamum, barley and clay; with this an infusion of a mixture of water with fish and flesh be made and all these are powdered to become a thick mash. The seed should be put at a depth of four digits and sprinkled with water mixed with fish and flesh. Trees should be planted under the influence of auspicious stars and planets.

4.4 Irrigation

The importance of irrigation was recognized by the Indian agriculturists and the kings and the ministers were alive to it.

An elaborate system of irrigation was devised. Terra-cotta ring wells constructed between 600 B.C. and 200 B.C. have been found in Hastināpur, New Delhi, Ropār, Ujjain, Mathurā, Nāsik and many places in South Bihar and eastern Uttar Pradesh.[76] Aśokan inscriptions refer to the construction of well at every *kos* on the highways.[77] Irrigation by water raised from wells, ponds, tanks, reservoirs and rivers by canals was a common practice. Water was raised and channelized by contrivances of wind-mills.[78] *Aparajita-prechchha* refers to irrigation from rivers and lakes, wells, *arahatta*, river dams etc. to avoid the dreadful effects of drought.[79] There are references to irrigaticn tanks, reservoirs etc. too. Kauṭilya lays down that a man who breaks a dam should be drawned. Manu also provides for similar punishments though he prescribes fine as well for such offence.[80] Manu advises remission of tax for five years if a man constructs tank or lake, and for four years altogether for improvement, restoration and extension of irrigation canals.[81]

Buddhist sources reveal that there are three types of engineers who constructed canals for irrigation of fields.[82] The Śakyas and Koliyas had built dams on the river Rohini.[83] Irrigation tanks, known as *cheruvo* or *keri* are mentioned in the South India inscriptions.[84] According to the Jain sources, Bāsavadatta is credited for construction of wells and tanks in Karnataka and traces of canals have been found in Nagarjunikonda.[85] Dr. Bhandarker is said to have found wells of canals in Vidiśā. Kālhana refers to restoration and repair of dams in Kashmir.[86]

The rulers and the ministers were alive to the utility of irrigation by state. We learn from the Hatigumpha inscription of Khāravela that a canal was constructed in Kalinga during the time of Nandas in Toshalinagar and the state took the responsibility of its maintenance.[87] Sudarśan lake constructed by Puṣyagupta during the time of Chadragupta Maurya restored and adorned by irrigation canals made by Rūdradamana, the vassal of the Gupta emperor Skandagupta.[88] It was repaired by Chakrapālita. Rulers of Kashmir, Harṣa, Siddharaj Jaisimha, Chalukyas of Gujarat and Karṇa took active interest in irrigation project.[89]

Tanks with brick walls dated between 600-200 B.C. built in north-west India for the monks and for irrigation purposes as well.[90] Epigraphic sources show that in 200 A.D. tanks were constructed in the western and south-western parts of India.[91]

4.5 Cattle Raising or Dairy Farming

The Āryans were a pastoral people to start with and as such, cattle was of much importance to them. In later period, agriculture assumed more importance, but the value of cattle did not diminish. Rather, cattle assumed immense economic value for ploughing, transport, food, hides, horns etc. Cows were specially valued for their milk and milk products like curds, clarified butter, fresh butter, butter milk and whey.[92] Hardly any ceremony could be held without milk or milk products. Cow-flesh, cow-bones and cow-dung were used for manuring and cow-dung also served as fuel.

Manu states that when the Lord of creation created the cattle, he handed it over for the *Vaiśya*.[93] Kamandaka also holds that cattle raising is the livelihood of the *Vaiśya*. But it was not the exclusive profession of the *Vaiśya*. King Dilip and his queen worshipped the cow of their *Guru* with sandle-paste and garland for getting a boon from her and Dilip used to take her out for tending.[94]

Ancient economy depended on cattle for cultivation, dairy products and transport. Cow, therefore, became a sacred animal and it is found in the literature. In Allahabad, on a pillar inscription, Samudragupta is said to have given thousands of cows for religious merit.

The slaughter of cow was considered as sinful as the murder of a *Brahamaṇa*.[95] Sanchi stone inscription of Chandragupta-II declares that whosoever shall interfere with the gift shall be invested with the sin of slaughter of a cow or a *Brahamaṇa*.[96] The Eran pillar inscription of Buddhagupta states: "Let property attend on all the subjects, headed by the cows and *Brahamaṇas*."[97]

Legal texts lay down rules for the protection of the cattle. If a cow does any mischief within ten days of calving, the owners shall not be liable to punishment.[98] He who employs at an improper time tired or hungry animals for drawing or carrying, shall be compelled to atone his offence in the same way as a cow-killer, or to pay the first fine.[99] Bullocks with dragging feet should not be used for carrying loads.[100] Moreover, when a man makes use of a cow without authorization from the owner, deserves the same punishment as a thief.[101] Nārada lays

28-29. *Ibid.*, XIII, p. 5.
30. R.C. Majumdar, *op. cit.*
31-33. *Amarkoṣa*, IX, p. 5.
32-35. *Ibid.*, pp. 9, 13, 14.
36. Cosmas, XI, p. 358.
37-40. R. Chowdhury, *op. cit.*, p. 101.
41. McCrindle, *op. cit.*, p. 54.
42. *Bṛhatsaṁhitā*, LV.
43-45. *Ibid.*, XIV, pp. 29-31.
46-47. S.K. Maity, *op. cit.*, p. 107.
48-58. *Ibid.*, pp. 109-111.
59. Cosmas, XI, p. 364.
60-61. S.K. Maity, *op. cit.*, p. 111.
62-67. *Bṛhatsaṁhitā*, LV, pp. 4-6.
68-70. S.K. Maity, *op. cit.*, p. 112.
71-73. *Bṛhatsaṁhitā*, LV, pp. 14-18.
74-75. *Ibid.*, LV, pp. 19-31.
76-86. R. Chowdhury, *op. cit.*, pp. 108-10.
87. R. Sharma, *op. cit.*, pp. 159-69.
88. *Epigraphica Indica*, VIII, p. 43.
89-91. R.S. Sharma, *op. cit.*, pp. 159-69.
92. S.K. Maity, *op. cit.*, p. 125.
93. *Manu*, IX, pp. 327-28.
94. *Raghu*, Canto II.
95-97. S.K. Maity, *op. cit.*, p. 125.
98. *Nārada*, XI, p. 30.
99-101. *Bṛhatsaṁhitā*, XXI, p. 21.
102-103. *Ibid.*, VII, pp. 10-13.
104. *Ibid.*, XXII, pp. 23-24.
105. *Nārada*, XI, p. 33.
106. *Matsya-Purāṇa*, p. 207.
107. *Bṛhatsaṁhitā*, LVI, pp. 5-19.

5

ARTS AND CRAFTS

India possesses abundant agricultural, forest and mineral resources. With these resources Indian people developed arts and crafts right from the dawn of civilization. These products of arts and crafts reached practically all over the civilized world and were in great demand. Thriving trade and commercial activities which we find reflected in her literature, art, architecture, sculpture and paintings.[1]

Urbanization, followed by localization and specialization of trade since 6th Century B.C., accelerated formation of guilds of artisans and craftsmen. Their skill perfected by heredity and apprenticeship helped the process of growth of industries. Though large scale industries were not developed, Indian craftsmen adopted mechanical devices, and invented and utilized tools to increase production.[2] Though in the Mauryan period crafts were highly regulated, in the classical literature, we do not find any reference to the state regulation of trade and commerce. With the growth of urbanization, production tended to be in the hands of *Vaiśyas* and these people were not regarded much in society.[3] This prevented perhaps, the growth of big industries and factories except the state-owned factories in the Maurya period. Mines were state monopolies and Kauṭilyan state strictly regulated and controlled production, even the guilds of craftsmen and artisans.[4] Most craftsmen engaged in metallic craft like copper, iron, lead, tin, silver, gold etc. did not possess metal but worked on those materials supplied to them by traders who controlled big business and they lived on wages paid by these traders.[5]

But arts and crafts began to develop from the end of Vedic Period, it is evident from the classical sources. A large number of arts, crafts, occupations and professicns are referred in the literature, epigraphs and sculptures. The Buddhist and Jain texts provide ample data on these developments. *Digha Nikya* mentions two dozens of trades but *Mahavastu* refers thirty six varieties of works. Milindapānho enumerated seventy five kinds of crafts.[6] Most inscriptions of western Deccan, Sānchi, Bhārhut, Mathurā, Bodhgayā refers to the donation of caves, pillars, tablets, cistern etc. to the Buddhist monks by weavers, dyers, goldsmiths, workers of ivory and metal, jewellers, sculptors, fishermen, smiths and perfumers.[7] Craft products of smith and weavers and ivory-workers were in great demand for long distance and export trade.[8]

That the craftsmen and artisans of India applied various mechanical devices and tools for their production is evident from *Arthaśāstra*.[9] Mechanization and heavy industry were deprecated by the orthodox class and very few crafts were exempted from stigma.[10] But, mechanical devices were developed and applied for irrigation projects, making ornaments, techniques for warfare, machines required for pressing sugar, oil, the water pump, or the hydaulic engines, for looms with shuttle and wheels and spokes.[11]

5.1 Mining and Metallurgical Industries

Mining and metal industries began to gain momentum from sixth century B.C. Kauṭilya[12] discusses the details of the process of mining which was a state monopoly. Possibly complete control over the mines and mineral was assumed by the state in appreciation with overall control and supervision of the operation of mines and *adhyakṣas* were appointed to supervise the production in different mines. The *Svarnadhyakṣa* controlled the production of gold, the *Lavaṇadhyakṣa* controlled the salt mines which were worked by private traders on payment of royalty; the *Suradhyakṣa* controlled distilleries and breweries.

The Chhotānāgpur area is the main source of metallic ores in north India and provided most of her gold, iron, mica etc. In industry, India developed a particular way of carbonization and Indian iron was executed in quality.[13] Development of iron and silver industries was a prerequisite of development of arts and crafts. For this reason, black-smiths occupied an important position among the artisans. Descriptions of villages of black-smiths of thousand families, with their furnaces and anvils, suggest that their industry was in a flourishing condition.[14] Iron was necessary for production of agricultural implements, like spades, sickles, ploughshares, chains, household tools, war weapons like swords, arrows, manufacture of tools like chisel, hammers etc. for artisans and craftsmen and even for improving means of communication and for building temples and houses. According to *Periplus*, Indian iron and steel products were so advanced that large quantities of them were exported to East

African countries.[15] Amongst the famous product of iron, the Mehrauli pillar which is made of wrought iron, measuring 23 feet in height and made in the Maurya period is a marvel of the world, it is still in existence withstanding the ravages of centuries. Iron beam were frequently used in the temples of Mathurā and Orissa and vessels of iron are also mentioned.[16] Iron objects have been found in Kauśāmbi, Benāras, Māson in Uttar Pradesh, Chirnad, Vaiśali, Patnā, Sonpur and Champā in Bihār.[17]

The art of copper and bronze casting had also attained a high water-mark of development in ancient India. Copper and bronze were used for making statue, utensils and coins. Copper statue of Buddha found in Sultanganj, figure of dancing girl, seated Buddha in bronze from Uttar Pradesh, one standing Buddha in Bronze from Bihar and another from Bheta near Allahabad, one standing female figure of copper, one copper basin, three tripods, one shallow saucer of copper, a cup of copper, one cooking pot in beaten copper, two bangles etc. have been found. Moreover, copper was used for making seals. Two seals have been found from Rajghat excavation site.[18] Gigantic copper statue of Buddha of eighty feet in height referred to by Hiuen tsang is one of marvels of metallurgical industries.[19] Besides these, the archaeologists discovered the craft of engraving letters on copper plate. It was a very technical art from most *grants* were engraved on copper plates. Copper was used for making seals also. Mostly copper and bronze were cast but in some cases these were beaten by hammering.[20]

Crafts of goldsmiths and jewellers had attained great importance for such products used by Indian people had an export market. People in India was fond of ornaments and both males and females decorated with jewels and ornaments are found in sculptures and painting specimens found in Buddhist monastries, *stupas* and caves as well as Hindu temples.[21] Jewels were used on ornaments for getting the favour of stars and good fortune as prescribed by Varāhamihira who mentions pearls of Ceylon, Persia and Pandya kingdom. *Bṛhatsaṁhitā* mentions twenty two varieties of jewels like diamonds, sapphire, emerald, moonstone, crystal, topaz, rubi etc. These are referred to in *Amarakoṣa*.[22] We have a vivid picture of jewellers work in *Mṛchhakatikam* by Śudraka.[23] Kauṭilya[24] enumerates diamonds of several varieties, the sources of which were Vidarbha, Kośala, Kāsi and Kalinga. Diamonds and precious stones were a speciality of the South.[25] Most of the gems and precious stones were used for making ornaments and inlay works by the jewellers. The jewellers enjoyed high social prestige in ancient India.

Glass making was an allied industry of metallurgy. People engaged in this craft were known as *Manikaras*. According to Coomaraswami, India had attained highest standard in this regard. And on the authority of Pliny, it can be said that it was without any parallel. Coloured glasses were known to Kauṭilya. Gopinath Rao holds that highly polished metal plates of various designs were used as mirrors in these days.[26] In a place called Aramula in Travancore such mirrors are still manufactured. According to Prof. Codrington, in the metal articles reorganized in Ajantā frescos are recognizable.[27] Newāri made copper and brass mirrors are still used in Tibetan villages.[28]

Salt making was also an important art. *Amarakoṣa* mentions two types of salts.[29] One from sea water and the other from the rock. The latter was unearthed from the mines and rock. It was a state monopoly as already mentioned and found at Māndi in Himachal and Kohār in Pakistan now. The first type was manufactured by drying up the sea water.[30]

Stone cutting and making stone statuary was also practised. Building pillars, columns, flight steps, irrigation works and sculptures were made of stones on large scale. Perfections attained in this regard are the Asokan pillars and inscriptions on stone, and rock temples and *stūpas*. A massive stone coffer of Mauryan time has been examined from the Piprawah *stūpa*, it contains a relic casket breaking *Brāhmi* inscription and another casket of berry has been found in Bhattiprolu.[31] Stone was also used for charter of Land Grants and Inscriptions as we see frequently in our study of economic history.

5.2 Agriculture Based Industry

Textile is one of the oldest industries in India. The art of manufacturing cotton by using the spinning wheel and loom is an ancient art. Pāṇini refers to weavers and villages of weaving the loom. The process of weaving was developed on intensive and extensive scales.[32] India was probably the first of all countries those perfected the weaving. We know that Gotami, the aunt of Buddha, undertook weaving.[33] Textile consisted of cotton, silk, wool, linen as well as bark of trees. Ajantā frescos reveal four distinct types of weaving.[34] The *abhiras* produced blankets of various qualities, blankets also came from Bahlika country.[35] Varanasi and Bengal were centres for textile industry and famous for their fine muslins.[36] Mathurā was known for its Sataka, which were exported.[37] Maheswamati, Mathurā, Konkan, Kalinga, Vanga, Ujjain were chief centres of cotton fabrics.[38] Mathura produced a fine striped variety of cotton cloth. Kauṭilya distinguishes three varieties of *Dakula* from Vanga, Pundra and Duvamakudya.[39]

Silk weaving was very important and guilds were organized by silk weavers. Mandasore inscription refers to building and repairing of a temple by a silk-weaver.[40] We read of silk weaver with a fine pattern of figures of swan in *Raghuvaṁsa*. Silk was used by the richer section of the society.[41] Silk was exported to foreign countries.

Dyeing was an ancillary of textile industry. In Trichirapally and Arkamedu brick built vats of 100-300 A.D. have been discovered which testify the existence of textile industry in the south.[42]

Embroidery was practised side by side with textile and dyeing crafts. In Ajanta paintings some coloured designs and embroidary have been found. Four techniques have been identified: *bandhana* or ordinary tie and dye work, double tied resin dyeing in which wrap and roof are dyed separately, before weaving according to the pattern requirement, brocading and fine muslin weaving.[43] The next prominent type of design are comparative bands alternately filled with geometric devices and cherrous, circles, checks etc. and formal motifs or schools.[44]

Production of oil from mustard seeds, sesamum, linseed, ingudī was another important agriculture based industry. Oilmen organized guilds for their common interest. Indore plate of Skandagupta refers to the famous guild of oilmen headed by Jīvanta.[45]

5.3 Industries Based on Forest Produce

Forests and gardens provided numerous varieties of wood, bamboo, canes, flowers, barks etc.[46] and forest animals produced silk, wool, skin, ivory, bones, horns, feathers etc.[47] On these, many crafts were developed. Carpentry was a popular and honourable profession in Vedic times.[48] Even *Brahmaṇas* were engaged in chariot making. There are references to wooden palaces, houses, city ramparts made of wood and other building activities in the *Jātakas*.[49] Wooden architecture was common in the Maurya period. Seven wooden pillars found in Kumhrar (Patna) and Jaimanlagadh (Begusarai) testify this.[50] There are references to wealthy carpenters, timber merchants, charioteers, wood-carvers and wood-architects. There is a reference in *Maha-umanga-Jātaka* that for repairing the rampart of the city of Mithilā, carpenters were sent to forest to bring the required timbers on three hundred boats.[51] Carpenters were also specialized in constructing boats and sea-going ships, carts and wooden furniture. Like timber, bamboo and canes were used for making and building household furniture. This is referred by Vatsayana as one of the sixty four crafts.[52] Fa-hien refers to five-storeyed bamboo structure upon a four wheel car used on festive occasion.[53]

Making of ivory products was also an important and lucrative craft. Ivory was used for making hair-combs, pins, dice, ornaments, swords, belts and miniature figurines which the wealthier people used and were exported to Western world.[54] Elephant tusks were imported from Africa to supplement the supply from indigenous forests. Gateway of Sanchi records the donation of ivory workers.[55]

Ship-building was an important forest-based industry. We hear of brink overseas trade of India right from the early centuries of Christian era. Mostly Indians used to carry on the maritime trade in their own vessels. Pliny refers to Indian ships which measured 3000 amphrose or seventy five tonnes.[56] In the fifth century, Fa-hien travelled from Tāmralipti to Ceylon and from latter country to Java in a ship carrying two hundred people with their cargo, besides the crew of the ship. The friezes of the Borobudur temple of Java and Ajanta paintings testify the shipping industries of ancient India.[57] Normally, the timber of the sea surfing vessels were not nailed or rivetted but slashed together, as sewn or lashed timbers were more resilient than nailed ones and could stand up better to the fierce storms of the monsoon and coral reefs of the Indian ocean.[58]

Wood-carving was a well-developed craft. Wooden masks, images, city gates and palaces were decorated with carved wooden panels. Fa-hien refers to an image of Buddha made by people of Darel on the western bank of Indus.[59] Chānakya mobilized all the carpenters of Pātaliputra to prepare the palace and city gates of the city for the entry of Chandragupta during the time of coronation.[60]

5.4 Soil Based Products

In ancient economy, making utensils, terra-cotta figures, seals and beeds and toys of clay were very important crafts.[61] The potters showed much skill and efficiency in moulding, burning and colouring pottery.[62] Generally pots or utensils were wheel-made, but moulded wares were also considerable in number. The excavation sites in different places, *viz.* Ahichhatra, Hastinapur, Kausambi, western Deccan and western India prove it.[63]

Pottery included cooking vessels of different sizes, different types of bowls and jars of different sizes, miniature bottles, dyeing vats used by the textile works. Besides these, stand for jar, goblet, *kamandalu* with cover and handle with two loops etc.[64] were also made. Many of these objects were decorated with various patterns such as rosettes, geometrical figures, bands of lotuses alternating with conches, running bears and elephants, designs in various shapes, *viz.* round ellipsoidal, flat-bottomed, open at the top and receding at the base.[65] Some drinking vessels bear beautiful handles of the pattern in ancient India. The most distinctive class of pottery, however, was what is usually called the *red-ware.*[66] This technique is said to have been imported to India from Mediterranean region.[67] But in many places of India this type was manufactured. An unique type of specimen is a jug found from Ahichhatra. It has a pinched spent, a loop handle twisted in imitation of a rope, a polished black surface and a black car.[68] According to Ghose and Pānigrahi, the characteristic of this jar which are alien to the indigenous potters' crafts must have been imported from Mediterranean region.[69] Along with this the potters made grey as well as black wares.[70] In some places of North India pots made of clay mixed with mica were manufactured.[71]

We may conclude potters craft with a reference to Ajantā frescoes. The most common pot shown in this is the spouted water jar, a type seen at Sānchi and Bhārhut brass reliefs.[72] The first is rounded-bottomed with a substantial rolled rim and a neck of varying length. Square pots of this type with wide mouth are represented in diminishing sizes to stack one upon the other. The second type is a rimmed foot and a long neck flaring outward at the mouth.[73] The ordinary drinking vessels seems to have been a shapely little cup, with a flat narrowly necked foot set out on a flat platter like dish.[74] The tray like dishes are often observed at Ajantā.

Next to utensils, the making of terra-cotta figures was very important.[75] In the modest medium of clay the moulders created things of real beauty. These must have been very cheap and have satisfied the need of poorer section of the people who could not afford to buy metallic or stone statuary which were costly. Terra-cotta figures were mostly of gods and goddesses but numerous figurines of ordinary men and women, different kinds of animal toys etc. were also manufactured. On festive occasions, these were in great demand.[76]

Terra-cotta showing playful lovers' scenes were placed in bedrooms. Figures of gods and goddesses, fishes, tortoises, crocodiles, coconuts, plantains and betel plants were kept in the houses for decoration purposes. At the time of Rājyaśrī's marriage a number of modellers were employed to manufacture these objects for decoration.[77] Classical literature refers to play objects or toys of terra-cotta. In *Śakuntalam*, Shakuntala's son is seen to play with a clay-made peacock and in *Mṛchhakatikam*, Rohasena, son of Chārudutta is seen playing a clay cart.[78]

Other important terra-cotta product was earthen beads.[79] Probably this was used by the poorer people as ornament to decorate their body as is done now-a-days by aborigins. Large specimen have been found in Ahichhatra.[80] These were sometimes coloured and painted.

Bricks made of clay was another avocation of ancient India.[81] Baked bricks have been found in many places of excavations. These were used for making walls of living houses, tanks and flight of steps in temples and other places.[82]

REFERENCES

1. R. Chowdhury, *op. cit.*, pp. 120-26.
2. *Ibid.*
3. *Ibid.*
4. *Ibid.*

5-8. R.S. Sharma, *op. cit.*, pp. 140-42.

9. R. Chowdhury, *op. cit.*, pp. 125-26.
10. *Ibid.*
11. *Ibid.*
12. *Ibid.*
13. *Ibid.*
14. *Ibid.*
15. *Ibid.*
16. R.S. Sharma, *op. cit.*, p. 155.
17. *A Cambridge History of India*, 3rd edn., Reprint, 1968, p. 122.

18-20. S.K. Maity, *op. cit.*, pp. 138-39.

21-24. R. Chowdhury, *op. cit.*, pp. 124-25.

25. *The Classical Age*, p. 596.

26-30. S.K. Maity, *op. cit.*, p. 128.

31. R. Chowdhury, *op. cit.*, p. 128.

32-39. *Ibid.*, pp. 123-25.

40. S.K. Maity, *op. cit.*, pp. 140-52.
41. *Ibid.*
42. R.S. Sharma, *op. cit.*, p. 142.

43-45. S.K. Maity, *op. cit.*, pp. 142-52.

46-51. R. Chowdhury, *op. cit.*, pp. 127-28.

52-53. S.K. Maity, *op. cit.*, pp. 149-50.

54-55. *Ibid.*

56-60. *Ibid.*, pp. 140-52

61-82. *Ibid.*, pp. 142-46.

6

TRADE AND COMMERCE

Trade and Commerce or movement of commodities both inside and outside the country are the main channels of distribution of the produce of a nation and uphold the social and the cultural fabric of a country. Therefore, a discussion of trade and commerce is essential for the study of the economic history of a country.

We have no definite idea about the evolution of market in India.[1] But reference to various types of markets are found in the epics. In the fairs and festivals, goods were bought and sold. The *Panyagṛha* of Kauṭilya mentions that in a market every house was earmarked for a particular merchandise. Aristobulus has referred to the market of Taxila where even prostitution was practised.[2] *Mahāumagga Jātaka* tells that there were three market towns in Mithila. Pliny refers to Udumbara, Pātaliputra and Champā as good market towns.[3] Thāneswar had good market where valuable merchandise from every quarters were exchanged, it is stated by Hiuen-tsang.[4] Bhṛgukachha and Ujjain were good market towns. In the south Pratisthana or Paithan of the Godāvari, there was an important trading centre.[5] Madura and Puhar were also important travelling centres.[6] There was an abundance of grains in Kānchi.[7] In Valabhi, rare and valuable products of different regions were available.[8]

It is possible that towns and markets developed in the holy places or places of pilgrimages also on the mouth of rivers or ports where sea-borne routes terminated or on the capital cities or other administrative centres of the provinces. Within the towns, localization of trade is found. For example, in Varanasi, there was an ivory workers street, the dyers and weavers had different places to trade and there was a *Vaiśya* street.[9] Also the villages developed as special market of different crafts, such as villages of woodwrights, iron-smiths, potters etc. They were the suburban to large cities and constituted special market for the whole countryside.[10]

The pastoral village culture of the *Aryans* gradually began to yield to urban culture and towns began to evolve from trade centres and craft villages. Localization of industry and creation of local market for the sale of products, however, resulted from the caste and guilds. Trades and commerce was generally conducted by the *Vaiśya* class. Considering the importance of their business, Kāmandaka advises the king to give the special privilege to the traders.[11] The importance of those people and prestige of merchants can be inferred from the fact that the *Nagaraśresthi* and guild merchants were included in the local administration. But in the later times, the *Brahmaṇas*, *Kṣatriyas* and *Śudras* were also in trade and commerce.[12]

However, trade in rural market was intra-local. It served the need of the local inhabitants. Craftsmen sold their commodities directly to their consumers. But trade in cities or urban centres was inter-local. The peasants surplus was in the hands of middlemen or a class of large merchants.[13] In urban centres, commodities were collected from many places. Inter-regional trade was an extension of inter-local trade. In the cities, commodities flew from villages to towns, in the former commodities allowed from town to town. In case of inter-local trade, commodities consisted of varieties of products. But in inter-regional trade both luxury and common food stuff were transferred to other regions where these were in demand. For example, sugar was transported to cooler and drier regions where cane would not grow well and rice was exported as luxury food to the parts of North-West.[14]

There are small as well as big merchants. The former generally satisfied the need of the local people. Big merchants collected commodities from centres of production and sent them to distant countries where they had their wholesale centres of production and sent them to distant countries where they had their wholesale agents. They distributed wares to retail dealers on share of profit or on commission basis.[15]

Caravan of traders travelled under a chief called *Sārthavāha*, for directions as to halt, watering, precaution against brigands, even as the routes.[16] The position of *Sārthavāha* was hereditary apparently. There was another common officer called *Sthalaniyamaka* who guided caravans through deserts and wastelands. We have evidence of merchants' caravan. I-tsing was accompanied on this journey from Tāmralipti to Bodhgayā by many hundred of merchants.[17]

6.1 Transport

Ox-driven carts were used for road transport. Ships and boats were put into services for water transport and by river boats, it was possible to go up to the Gangā to Shreyate and up the Jamuna to Kosāmbi.[18] Further westward the journey overland proceeded to Sind from where came large import of horses and asses and to Sorbia and its ports.[19] There is reference to a class of small shippers confined to inland navigation.[20]

Ships were large enough to carry 500 to 700 passengers with their cargos. The *Bṛhatsaṁhitā* refers to the existence of shippers and sailors whose health is said to be influenced by the moon.[21] There is reference to ship-owners who has become wealthy by constantly levying freight in some seaport town, will be able to travel the high seas and go to Vanga or Takkola or China or Souvira or Surat or Alexandria or the Coromandel coast or further India or many other places where ships congregate.[22, 23] Kālīdāsa mentions that both land routes and waterways served the purpose of transport.

Elaborate rules were provided in the law books for transportation of goods.[24] When a merchant hires a transport or labour of transportation of commodities and other party fails to do the job; adequate compensations were to be made. But, if the former does not use it, he will have to make good the wage or rent.

To encourage, promote and facilitate trade, both inland and foreign, states were enjoyed to improve and increase means of communication and transport.[25] Rest houses and store houses were to be provided for traders and police escorts were to be provided for security against thieves, robbers and forest tribes. Many of the trade routes passed through dense jungles and over hills. There were villages of professional robbers ready to way lay the merchants. Besides there were dangers from wild beasts, like tigers, elephants and snakes. Under these circumstances, merchants travelled together in caravans, guarded by professional caravan guards.[26] To encourage imports, suitable rebates were granted to foreign traders, if current rates did not have a proper margin of profit for them.[27] Indigenous merchants were encouraged to seek new market for the surplus produce of the country.[28] Foreign merchants could sue in Indian courts and were protected from being harassed by suits against them in local courts.[29]

The Mauryan emperor encouraged overseas trade to the diplomatic missions; exchange of envoys between Greek kings of Western Asia and Egypt and the Mauryan is on record.[30] Close relation between Aśoka and Tissa, the king of Ceylon, must have resulted in close trade between the two countries.

6.2 Market

Elaborate rules were formed for organization, establishment and management of market, to prevent speculation and smuggling.[31] Adulteration, cheating and dishonest dealing were punishable according to the quality of the offence, with fine, imprisonment and even mutilation. Bṛhaspati and Nārada have put down rules for benefits of both the sellers and consumers. Sale was to the public, nothing could be bought from imbecile or an unauthorized seller. If a man was cheated, he was to be compensated. Articles could be returned if the purchaser felt that he had made a bad bargain.[32]

6.3 Prices

The *Jātaka* stories mention that prices were settled by haggling, competitions and customs. The state did not control the prices except for its own purchase.[33] It had its own value and was offered bribes by the merchants to secure high prices. In the Mauryan empire, the state controlled prices, as stated by Megasthenes which is corroborated by *Arthaśāstra*.[34]

Prices were generally fair, the *Amarkoṣa* refers business deeds showing description of commodities purchased and also ratifies bargain.[35]

In the classical period, however, there was no regulation of prices by the state. But in the Maurya period, state controlled the price.[36] Kauṭilya advocates considerable state control both in trade and industry. It was obligatory on traders to get a licence, while the foreign traders were required a passport in addition.

It is interesting to observe that ancient Indian economists had a fair conception of the fundamental causes of value.[37] According to Kauṭilya's *Arthaśāstra* two factors were to be considered in fixing value of prices. They are: (i) the cost of production in determining supply, and (ii) the demand of the article as determined by its utility. Even writers of the *Smṛtis* correctly understood the causes of values, as is seen in Manu's precepts for the guidance of the king in fixing the rates of duty.[38] References to absolute and relative prices are found in *Sūtras* and the Buddhist works.

In the Mauryan period, the whole sale prices were fixed by the superintendent of commerce as they passed the custom house.[39] A margin of profit was allowed to the retailers. The public consumers and customers were protected by the state, which employed an army of spies and market inspectors. Goods had to be sold at fixed market places and dealers had to specify particulars as to the quality, quantity and price which were scrutinized and recorded in the official books. The superintendent of commerce was to ensure that the material, its quantity and measure corresponded to the terms bargained.[40]

Commodities were measured properly, both by length and weight and values were known.[41] Linear measurement was resorted for measurement of height or length of commodities. Prices and weights were varied from place to place. Such units as *pala, prastha* etc. are referred to in the literary sources.

Kauṭilya advocates state monopoly of industry on the basis of risk, cost or variety.[42] The state was advised to become both the manufacturer and trader and to sell the articles through departmental agencies. Mines, comprising those of gold, copper, lead, tin, iron, bitumen which provided the main sources of state revenue were nationalized. Pearl, mother of pearl, conch shell, coral etc. were explored from ocean mines and it was a state concern. Ores provided minerals while *rasa* like mercury came from the oil fields. Salt manufacture was a state monopoly for licences were granted to the private lessees of salt-fields. There was also state monopoly of ornament industry, coinage and ship building. Further, the state controlled the manufacture and sale of wines and liquor. Cotton, oil and sugar factories were also state concerns.[43]

Prison factories, worked through penal labours added to the state produces.[44] Yearns of cotton, wool, silk and jute came from the state spinning factories which manufactured clothing of all types, coat of mail, blankets, curtains and ropes. For spinning yarn, helpless women were employed under women supervisors.[45]

Trade required easy availability of medium exchange, *i.e.* money. It appears that uninscribed punchmark metallic currency had become regular feature of economic life by the sixth century B.C. Thousands of such coins have been unearthed from different parts of the country.[46] The earliest coins of silver and copper were based on the weight system of *Manusmṛti*. *Suvarṇa* was the standard gold coin of 80 *ratis* based from the time of Kuṣaṇas, while copper coin of the same weight was called *Karsapāna*. *Purāṇa* or *Dharana* of 32 *ratis* was a silver coin and copper coin of 100 *ratis* was called *pāna*. Specimens are available to show that the king, the guilds and even merchants issued coins duly stamped signifying the correctness, weight and purity of the metal.[47]

6.4 Trade Routes

In the sixth century B.C. trade routes covered most of the northern India and by the Maurya times similar routes existed in the peninsula.[48] Among the chief of these was one which lay from Tāmralipti up to the Gangā to Champā and then through Pātaliputra, Vārānasī to Kauśāmbī whence a branch went to the port of Bhṛgukachchha on the mouth of Narmadā by the way of Vidiśā and Ujjain. The main road passed by the modern Delhi and crossed the five rivers of Punjāb by way of Sākāla (Śialkot) to the north-western city of Taxila where it continued up the Kabul valley and on to the Central Asia.[49] From Mathurā a branch went to the port of Patalo, on the mouth of Indus.[50]

The main routes from northern places to the south had laid across the *Vindhyas* more or less through western section of the latter. A route went to the south from Ujjain to the city of Pratisthāna, the capital of Sātavāhana empire. There it passed across the Deccan plateau to the low Kṛṣṇā and went to Kāverī and Mādurai. A network of roads developed linking this route to all the important cities of the peninsula. There was a route which lay along the Mahānadī valley, from the neighbourhood of Vārānasī, Mirzapur, Allahabad through Chhattisgarh plains and then along the narrow gorge of Mahānadī until it opened into the delta at its eastern end.[51] The last route from north to south lay along the eastern coastal plain stretching from the south-western confines of Bengal down to Kāverī delta in the extreme south. This was a most difficult route in the past.[52] The western routes were more important and many of them down the peninsula had their focal points in the west.[53] the centres of the empire of the Sātavāhana and western *Kṣatrapas* were located in the west and the port of the Vijaynagar empire was in the same neighbourhood.[54] Nevertheless, the Chola and Gajapati emperors had their centres in the east and the Chālukya and Rāṣtrakūta empire had their focal points in the centre.[55]

Early Buddhist text, like the *Jātakas* and *Niddas*, the *Periplus of the Erythrian sea* and Ptolemy's geography, recorded the existence of many harbours, ports and market towns all along the eastern and western coasts which were the seats of trade from very early times between India and the Western countries. In the neighbourhood of the Gulf of Cambay, lay the port of the sea and a road which ran from this point through the high lands of Malwa on to the plains of the Gangā.[56] The ports through which the trade with western Asian countries and Europe was carried on in the past were Broach, Conkan and Surat.[57] From these ports, the north-eastern roads followed through the Chambal and Betwa valley.[58] Many of the Buddhist and Brahmaṇical monasteries were situated in this route joining and combining the Gangā.

Similar route from Calicut to the Coromandel coast lay through the hills and gap of Palghat. Trade of this prosperous region was either focused at this point or was carried on by negotiating the northern and southern trades of the high lands of Kerala.[59]

On the eastern shores of the peninsula lay many ports, trade with Burma, Indonesia, Thailand and China was carried from these ports which were well connected with the main land routes.[60] Periplus mentions an important point of embarkation at the mouth of the Gangā, called Gangā, generally identified as Tāmralipti from where Fa-hien left for China *via* Ceylon (presently Sri Lanka).[61]

India's trade with the outside world thus carried both by land and sea routes.[62] The link between the major trade centres of population on Eurasian continent dates back to at least the days of Persian empire of the Achemaenians. There was a route through the Khyber Pass to the upper Kabul valley and then across the Hindukush to Balkh on the highway connecting the east and the west. Several routes radiated from Balkh towards China and Central Asia on the east and two to the West. Two more routes passed *via* Kandahar, one joining the above route at Herāt, while the other proceeded to Persepolis and Susa. There were yet two more routes to China[63], one through upper Burma to the south-western provinces of China (Tonkein to Wamsup) and another all sea route along the islands of East Indies. Hiuen-tsang started from Indies in A.D. 629. He came to Samarkand and proceeding along the bank of Oxus, reached Bokhara and Tarmuz and then to Bālkh and travelling further south, he came to Baiyan and from there to Kāfristan and Kāsmir. In the east a rout connected Pundravardhana with Kāmrup.[64]

6.5 Foreign Trade

From the accounts of Cosmas and others we know that main ports were Sindhu, Orhatha (Gujarāt), Calliana (Kālyana), Sibor (Chenwal), Tāmralipṭi and a few others. All these ports maintained regular trade with Ceylon, Persia, Ethiopia, the Byzantine empire, China and then the islands of Indian Ocean.[65]

From earliest times India has flourishing trade relations with Ceylon which was known as Tāmbaparṇī.[66] Its strategic position gave it an importance and it served as an entry point. Traders coasting around India from Bhṛgukachchha in the west went to Suvarnabhūmi in the east *via* Ceylon. I-tsing saw many Persian ships which traded with India and China and visited many islands of Southern Asia.[67]

Ceylon received silk, aloes, cloves, sandal woods and other products. Indian elephant which were sold by cubic measurement and horses found good market in Ceylon.[68] Varāhamihira mentions the import of Ceylonese pears and gems into India.[69] *Rājtarangini* mentions the import of Ceylonese cloth in India.[70] Perhaps silver was also imported into India from Ceylon as the metal was scarce in India.

India's commercial relationship with China was also flourishing.[71] The chronical of Sung Chu mentions that all the precious things of the land coming to China was from India. Gems made of Rhinoceros horns, King fishers' stones, serpent pearls and asbestos clothes and many other things were imported into China from India. Potic (fine cloth), a fine textile also found market in China. Chinese silk and a few other articles were imported into India from China. India also maintained a close trade relationship with the islands between India and China such as Champā, Borneo, Bālī, Cambodia, Sumātrā and others and with the Malay peninsula and Burma.[72] Mainly spices were brought home from these islands.

Earlier centuries of the Christian era witnessed the growth of brisk trade between India and the West, with the Roman empire as the chief customer.[73] There was a large volume of sea-trade between India and Western countries as far as African coasts. From the coast, the goods were carried by land to the Nile, and then down the river to Alexandria which was a great emporium. There was great demand for Indian manufactures and luxury goods, such as precious stones and pearls, scents, spices and perfumes, silk and textile goods. Roman dames dressed in seven folds of Indian muslin paraded the streets and became such a menace to the morales that the Senate intervened and laid an embargo on the import of that fine clothes from India.[74] Pliny, the Roman historian, bewails fifty millions of Sesterces, *i.e.* gold coins being drained out annually to pay for Indian imports.[75] During the reign of Justinian, silk was very costly in the Romān empire. The merchants held that they had to purchase the item at an exorbitant price from Perisan traders and pay heavy custom duty. But Justinian fixed the price of silk eight pieces of gold per pound.[76] In fact, silk and spices had become articles of daily use in the houses of Romān nobles. An evidence of flourishing trade between India and Rome is furnished by the fact that when Aleric spared Rome in A.D. 408, he obtained 3,000 pounds of pepper as a part of ransom.

In his register, Justinian mentions the following items of foreign trade.[77] Indian iron not liable to corrosion, Indian perfume, pearls, Sardonyx, Ceraunimum, Jacinth, diamond, sapphire, turquoise, beryl, tortoise sheels, various Indian opiates, raw silk, silk or half silk robes, silk yarn, Indian eunuchs, pradi, leopard and panthers, cinnamon, peppers, white pepper, costus (an aromatic plant), costamomum, spike-ward, ginger, malabathrum (betel), cardamom, cinnamon wood and ivory. Most of these commodities were possibly imported from India.

After the fall of Rome, India's trade relation continued with eastern Roman Empire or Byzantine, coins of this empire of fourth, fifth and sixth centuries have been found in east-south and western India.[78]

The representation of ships and boats at Ajantā offered a vivid testimony of foreign trade and ship-buildings which are corroborated by contemporary literary works.[79] The *Bṛhatsaṁhitā* refers to the existence of ship-builders and sailor as a class whose health is said to be influenced by the moon.[80] From the accounts of Cosmas we know that India had maritime relations with Ethiopia.[81] From Ethiopia, however, India imported emeralds, tusks and many kinds of spices, frakincense, cassia, calamus and many other articles as are known from the accounts of Cosmas.[82] India also imported horses from Arabia and Persia. Periplus mentions Indian trade relation with Doubias, a district in Persermenia.

Medium of exchange in China trade was perhaps, China silk, because we find no Chinese coins in India.[83] In case of trade with all eastern countries Roman coins were used. As many as 612 gold coins and 1187 silver coins have been discovered in South India, some 55 per cent being from Coimbatore and Madurai districts.[84] Coins of north India were largely melted by Kuṣaṇas. Yet some coins of Rome between Augustus and Nero have been found in the Hazara district of Punjab.

Economic prosperity of ancient India was largely due to its foreign trade. Indian traders ventured in all direction from Central Asia to China, to West Asia and South-East Asia. They became middlemen in the commerce between South-East Asia and the Mediterranean and supplied the need and luxuries of Greek-Roman nobles. But in comparison with other periods Gupta India witnessed a great expansion of foreign trade and commerce; perhaps the western drive of Samudragupta completed by Chandragupta-II was inspired by the desire to occupy West.[85] Moreover, trade relations with these countries affected the culture of India as well as of those countries which came in contact with India. India stood as the heart of Asia and maintained her position as one of the foremost maritime countries in the ancient world.

Thus we find that in ancient India trade and commerce flourished in almost all parts of the country. India had developed inland trade and traders deposited their goods to ports on call for foreign trade. India's maritime trade had assumed greater proportion. She imported goods for export with her indigenous products. This must have brought in wealth from oversea countries and the balance of trade must have been in her favour.

REFERENCES

1-8. R. Chowdhury, *op. cit.*, p. 166.
9-10. *Cambridge History*, p. 185.
11. *Kamandaka*, V, pp. 78-79.
12. M.L. Bose, "Social Change and Professional Mobility in Ancient India", published in *Journal of Historical Research*, Vol. V, 1994.
13-14. A.L. Basham, *op. cit.*, pp. 218-28.
15. R.C. Majumdar, *op. cit.*, p. 146.
16. A.L. Basham, *op. cit.*, p. 227.
17. R.C. Majumdar, *op. cit.*, p. 507.
18-20. *The Cultural Heritage*, p. 660.
21-23. A.L. Basham, *op. cit.*, pp. 228-29.
24. *The Classical Age*, pp. 601-02.
25. *The Cultural Heritage*, Vol. II, p. 669.
26. A.L. Basham, *op. cit.*, p. 227.
27-30. *The Cultural Heritage*, Vol. I, p. 40.
31-32. S.K. Maity, *op. cit.*, pp. 163-64
33. *The Age of Imperial Unity*, p. 600.
34. A.L. Basham, *op. cit.*, pp. 216-17.
35. *The Age of Imperial Unity*, p. 600.
36-40. *The Cultural Heritage*, Vol. II, p. 660.
41. S.K. Maity, *op. cit.*, p. 167.
42-45. *The Cultural Heritage*, Vol. II, p. 600.
46-47. *The Vakataka Gupta Age*, p. 295.
48-49. A.L. Basham, *op. cit.*, pp. 226-27.
50. *Ibid.*
51-65. *The Cultural Heritage*, pp. 5-6, 444-46.
66-72. S.K. Maity, *op. cit.*, pp. 170-71.
73. R.C. Majumdar, *op. cit.*, p. 212.
74. *The Age of Imperial Unity*, p. 603.
75. R.C. Majumdar, *op. cit.*, p. 213.
76. *The Classical Age*, p. 637.
77-78. S.K. Maity, *op. cit.*, pp. 176-78.
79-82. R.C. Majumdar, *op. cit.*, p. 177.
83-85. *The Classical Age*, p. 635.

7

GUILDS AND PARTNERSHIPS

That the organization of the guilds dates back to the end of the Vedic period can be inferred from the mention of *Gaṇa*, *Pūja*, *Vṛata* and *Saṁha* by Pāṇini.[1] The terms *Gaṇa* and *Saṁgha* were used to mean union for political and other purposes while *Pūja* and *Śreṇī* signified organization of merchants, artisans and others whose principal object was to gain wealth by trade and industry.[2] The *Dharma-sūtras* indicate that the chief industries were all organized in guilds. By the time of Buddhists two types of guilds, namely, industrial and commercial or professional came into being. Literature provide very little information about the constitution of these guilds of workers and craftsmen. Possibly guilds corresponding to the modern labour organizations and Merchants' guilds approximated to the Guild Merchant of medieval Europe.[3] The guilds effectively controlled local sources of production, arts and crafts, trades and industries and served as an important link between the central authority and the several economic units in the country.[4]

The guilds were autonomous, they taxed themselves, and they were competent to proceed with any lawful undertaking and to do things not prejudicial to the state interest.[5] The king was, of course, enjoined to restrain the illegal, immoral, indecent and seditious activities of those organizations. By the time of Kauṭilya, the *Saṁghas* and *Śreṇīs* had become very rich and powerful and some of them maintained troop of their own.[6] The potential danger to the state from the unstrained power of these organizations seem to underlie the severe regulations of these in the *Arthaśāstra*.[7] By the time of Guptas, *Saṁghas* and guilds had acquired immense power and status and had come to play a very vital role in the economic life of the country.

There are different kinds of guilds. The *Jātaka* stories specified sixteen unspecified *Śreṇīs* or crafts-guilds under the chief called *Pramukha*.[8] *Arthaśāstra* mentions *Saṁghas* and *Gaṇas* organized under

Mūkhiyas.[9] In the *Raghuvaṁsa*, a guild of architects is found; Mūdrārākṣasa refers to a guild of jewelers; Nāsik cave inscription refers a guild of weavers; the Indore stone inscription mentions a guild of oilmen; the Māndasor inscription refers to a guild of silk weavers.

Guild was formed by an agreement among the intending members and they were obliged to abide by its terms. Mutual confidence having first been established by means of sacred libation, by stipulation in writing or by umpires they shall set about their works.[10] A contract formed amongst the villages, companies or artisans and associations is called an agreement. An agreement was to be executed to provide against dangers and for the purpose of discharging their duties.[11] The executive of the guilds was to consist a president who was assisted by two or three members.[12] A person who was educated and honest and conversant with the *Vedas* and coming from a respectable family was selected as the president.[13] The executive officers were ultimately responsible to the assembly.[14] According to Nārada regular rules were laid down for attendance of members in the assembly.[15] There were guild hall for transaction of business and affairs of the guilds. The guilds had legislative, executive, legislature and judicial functions and even the family matter of the members were adjudicated by the guilds, says Gautama.[16] Guilds could deal with the offending members and punish one who disobeyed their decision, punishment varying from mild censure to expulsion.[17] The king could intervene only if the decision of the guild was not in conformity with the charter of the guild.[18]

Bṛhaspati states whatever is done by these heads of associations, whether harsh or kind to the other people in accordance with the prescribed regulation, must be approved by the king.[19]

Yājñavalkya holds that a man who steals the property of the guild and breaks the agreement should be banished from the realm and all his property shall be confiscated. He further lays down that a guild can possess corporate property and lay down rules and regulations for its guidance.[20]

Democratic feature in the guild organization is quite apparent; three characteristics of the guild were[21]: (i) pursuit of father's possession by son, (ii) localization of industries, and (iii) leadership of *Jethaka* or *pramukha*. The guilds, however, provided scope for development of skill and ingenuity of the individual members and safeguarded the local craft investment. Each guild usually had a tutelary deity of its own.[22]

Guilds became not only the basis of the production and distribution of merchandise but also the financial centres of trade. The Sātvāhanas, for instance, often gave to religious charities donations which came from the money invested with guilds.[23] Devaviṣṇu deposited *dīnñras* for maintenance of a lamp in the Sun-temple of Indore.[24] With accumulation of wealth in the hands of the guilds and merchants, patronage of learning and arts was no long confined to royalty. Many magnificent Buddhist monuments owe their existence to the donations of wealthy guilds and merchants.[25] *Stūpas* of Sānchi, Bhārhut and Amarāvati testify that. A guild of silk weavers built a magnificent temple and repaired it in A.D. 38.[26] Bṛhaspati mentions philanthropic activities of the guilds.[27]

In post-Maurya times, first evidence of the guild of artisans is found in 2nd century A.D. In Sātavāhana territory, oil millers, weavers, flour makers deposited silver *pānas* to the chief of a guild for 100 monks and *Brāhmaṇas* to be fed.[28] Guilds undertook their corporate authority works of social utility, such as construction of shelters for travellers, provision for drinking water, temples, pools, gardens and extended their helping hand to people in performing *Saṁskaras*.[29]

7.1 Partnership

The *Jātakas* refers to the merchants' partnership. Usually the caravans of the traders are found to be travelling together only for mutual benefit, like safety and security and even avoidance of mutual under selling.[30] The cultivation of the soil and various other arts and crafts were also carried on by workers on the basis of partnership.[31]

The *Smṛti* of pre-Gupta and Gupta period added a new head of law called *Sambhuya Samuthāna* or business in partnership.[32] Under this head, Manu extends the rule relating to the shares of the fees payable to the priests jointly performing a sacrifice, to all those who similarly do their work jointly.[33] On the other hand, Yājñavalkya applies the law of partnership in trade to the sacrificial priests, the businessman and artisans.[34] The clauses relating to the division of profits among the partners as well as their rights and duties are marked by equity and good sense.

The division of profit and loss among the partners in trade should be in proportion to their share in the business of agreement arrived at in this regard.[35] The division of profit among four grades of artisans, namely the apprentice, the advanced student, the expert and the master craftsman is to be in proportion of 1:2:3:4. Among the builders of palaces the local architect receives double his share of profit (Bṛhaspati and Kātyayan).

A partner doing work that is forbidden or causing harm through negligence is to make good the loss, while who preserves the property from a calamity is to get that as his award.[36] A partner is unable to do his job himself may get it done by an agent but he who follows other ways should be deprived of his profit and expelled.[37]

The *Smṛti* law provides the business in partnership among architects, masons and carpenters. *Medhātithi* says that the wages are to be distributed on the principle that he who has done the more difficult part of the job gets more and he who does the easy part gets the less. Partnership according to *Smṛti-Chandrika* are of six kinds, of which the first three are concerned with trade, agriculture and crafts.[38] Among merchants, profits and loss as well as expenditure and work are divided by the partners according to the capital laid out by each: alternately profit and loss were to be shared made by the parties.[39] This rule applied to cultivators as well. Craftsmen rule: gold smiths shared according to the nature of work, 1:2:3:4, the master craftsmen received double the share in building activities.[40]

As success of partnership largely depends upon the members who constitute the association, Bṛhaspati clearly stresses the necessity of selecting partners.[41] He suggests that partnership should not be carried by prudent men jointly with incompetent or large number of persons or with persons such as afflicted by illness, ill-fated or destitutes. On the other hand, a man should carry on business jointly with good persons as clever, active, intelligent, familiar with coins, skilled in revenue and expenditure, honest and enterprising.[42]

The relationship of individual members with the whole group is clearly laid down by Nārada and Bṛhaspati. The latter says that whatever one partner may give or lend authorized by many or whatever contract be may cause to be executed, all that is considered as having been done by all.[43] But when a single partner acting without the assent of other partners or their expressed injunctions, injures their joint property through his negligence, he must himself give a compensation to all his partners.[44] When one partner is found to have practiced deceit in a purchase or sale, he must be cleared by oath or ordeal.[45] The partners themselves are pronounced to be arbitrators and witnesses for one another in doubtful cases, and when fraudulent act has been discovered, unless a previous case should exist between them, they have the power to adjudicate it.[46] King could intervene if the wrong doer deals that injustice has been made to him. On the other hand, if the property of the partnership is preserved by exertion of one member from ill-fate, gang of robbers or through the king, he should get a tenth part of it or goods shall belong to him.[47]

The corporate body looked after the interest of the members even after their death. Bṛhaspati[48] states that if any partner in trade happens to die through want of proper care, his goods must be shown and delivered to the officers appointed by the king. If anyone comes to claim that man's property as heir to the deceased partner he has to prove his claim by the evidence of the other people and then only he can get it. In such cases, however, the king shall take one-sixth out of the property of *Śudra*, *Vaiśya*, *Ksatriya* and *Brāhmaṇa*. But, if nobody claimed the property of the person within three years, the king shall appropriate the property. The property of a *Brāhmaṇa*, however, was to be bestowed on another *Brāhmaṇa*.[49]

Another good effect of partnership was in the due discharge of works, for at the sudden death or incapacity of one partner the general work of the corporation did not suffer unduly. Nārada states that if one partner met with an accident, his heir should replace him, or on the failure of an heir, another man, or all the partners, if they are capable of becoming his substitute[50], would replace him. In the same way, among several persons jointly performing a ceremony, if anyone should meet with an accident, his part in the ceremony shall be performed by a kinsman of his or all by his associates in the work.[51]

REFERENCES

1. R. Chowdhury, *op. cit.*
2. *The Classical Age*, pp. 603-04.
3. A.L. Basham, *op. cit.*, p. 220.
4. *Ibid.*
5. *The Classical Age*.
6. A.L. Basham, *op. cit.*, p. 220.

7-9. *The Cultural Heritage*, Vol. II, pp. 674-75.

10-11. *Bṛhaspati*, XVII, pp. 7-13.

12. *The Classical Age*, p. 605.

13-15. R. Chowdhury, *op. cit.*, pp. 201-05.

16. *Gautama*, XI, p. 21.

17-18. R. Chowdhury, *op. cit.*

19. *Bṛhaspati*, VII, p. 18.

20. *Yājñavalkya*.

21-22. R. Choudhury, *op. cit.*, pp. 201-05.

23. *The Cultural Heritage*, Vol. II, pp. 674-75.

24. R. Choudhury, *op. cit.*, p. 201.

25. *The Cultural Heritage*, Vol. II, p. 45.

26-27. R. Choudhury, *op. cit.*, p. 201.
28. R.S. Sharma, *op. cit.*, p. 142.
29. R. Choudhury, *op. cit.*, p. 201.
30-31. *The Cultural Heritage*, Vol. II, p. 674.
32. *Bṛhaspati*, XIII; *Nārada*, III, pp. 1-9.
33-37. *The Cultural Heritage*, Vol. II, pp. 674-75.
38-40. *Ibid.*, p. 677
41-42. *Bṛhaspati*, XIII, pp. 1-3.
43. *Ibid.*, XIII, p. 22.
44. *Ibid.*, XIII, p. 9; *Nārada* III, p. 5.
45. *Ibid.*, XIII, p. 7.
46. *Ibid.*, p. 6.
47. *Ibid.*, p. 11; *Nārada*, III, p. 6.
48. *Ibid.*, XIII, pp. 14-16.
49. *Ibid.*
50. *Nārada* III, p. 7.
51. *Bṛhaspati*, XIII, p. 18; *Nārada*, III, p. 8.

8

LABOUR

Labour is one of the four means of production. That its due importance was fully appreciated by the ancient writers on economics is attested by the works of Kauṭilya, Kāmandaka, Śukra and others, though a dismal picture has been painted by *Smṛtis* on the basis of possibly the Buddhist works. According to Śukra, the remuneration of the labourer should be proportional to his productivity and qualification, and the wages should be sufficient to maintain the labourer and his family in tolerable comfort.[1] He also holds that there should be provisions for leisurely hours, leave and bonus for domestic servants and workmen's insurance for sickness, old-age and accidents. The writers on labour hold that hired labour cannot be abolished and efficiency results from training. Of course, they maintain that workmen are incapable of conducting industry and supervisory authority was necessary for getting work done and proper output can be ensured only through payments by result.[2]

8.1 Slavery

Slaves constituted an important segment of the labour force of ancient India. That is existed in some forms is evident not only from indigenous sources like the epics and the *Smṛtis*, but even secular Sanskrit literature, Buddhist and Jain canonical literature and the inscriptions of ancient India establish this fact. Of course, slave markets are not mentioned in early sources but in the early centuries of the Christian era, there was trade of slave-girls between India and the Roman empire in both directions.[3] The *Smṛtis* not only distinguish between different classes of slaves but lay down various rules regarding their status. There was, however, no caste of slaves.

The Sanskrit word *dāsa* has been translated into English as 'slave'. The origin of the word, however, is doubtful and its use as synonym of slave is possibly not proper. The word *dāsa* meant a number of people conquered by the Āryans. Definitely, in Indian history, there is no evidence to prove that the entire conquered people or tribes were condemned into slavery[4], and servitude was exacted from such people, as was the case in ancient Egypt or Mesopotamia or even in the Roman empire.[5] Of course, it is quite possible that some people captured in battle were taken into slavery and they were styled as *dāsa*. The *Mahābhārata* declares that it is a law of work that vanquished should be the victor's slave, and the captive would serve his captor until ransomed.[6] These people were also designated as *dāsa*. Hence, there is the confusion.

Whatever might have been the origin of slavery, with the progress of Indian civilization, it was systemized as an institution and both the *Smṛtis* and the *Arthaśāstra* categorized them according to their term of servitude. *Arthaśāstra* divides the slaves into five classes.[7] *Dhvajhrta* or those who were captured in the battle; *ātmavikrayin* or those who sold themselves in slavery; *undaradasa* or one born to a master from his *dāsi* or slave woman; *ahitaka* or one who could not pay for his debt; and finally *daṇdapranita* or one condemned to slavery by the judgement of court. Many mention seven kinds of slaves, *viz.* one captured in the battle, one who sells himself for food, one born in the house of a slave man, one bought, one given, one inherited and one who is condemned by the court.[8]

In all the *Smṛtis*, the author Nārada gives an exhaustive treatment of the institution of slavery.[9] He enumerates fifteen kinds of slavery. Those who were captured in the battle unless ransomed were slaves; those who survived the death of the master passed on to the legitimate heirs as slaves; children born to the slaves of the master were *Gṛhaja* or *udaradāsa*; those who were purchased from the market were *kṛtdāsa*; slaves could be held in mortgage; a person having religious order according to Nārada, was slave, those who could not maintain themselves could themselves up for maintenance and they could become slaves; a debtor could become a slave to any for his debt to his creditor; there were others who voluntarily accepted slavery either for penance or to free somebody; slaves could be had through wager; somebody having sexual relations with a female slave becames temporarily a slave to the master of that female slave; one could become a slave for a stipulated period, and finally, one could sell himself into slavery.

In the earlier period, possibly the slaves were engaged in agricultural works but gradually slaves were engaged only in domestic works. Nārada again divided domestic works under two heads: pure and impure.[10] The following works were to be performed by the slaves only: sweeping the gateway, the privy, the road and the place for rubbish. Massaging the secret parts of the body, cleaning the food remains, odour and urine were the impure works to be performed by the slaves. Washing the feet of the master after his return to home was the duty of maidservant.

The master of the slave could let out the services of their slave on hire; slave girls could be let out for sexual enjoyment, the offspring being accepted as interest.[11] Of course, a slave girl could not be enjoyed without proper authorization but enjoyment without permission amounted to five or two *pānas* for a day, as fine.

The slave did not have any right as he was not his own master. He was not that way much better than his master's chattel. The master had the right to recover his slave if he did run away or gave himself to somebody else. The master had the right to pledge him or give him up to another person. A slave could not own any property legally, for all that he earned belonged to his master.[12] A slave could not stand as a witness unless there was no other available and transaction of a slave, unless authorized duly, was invalid.[13]

Most of the slaves depended entirely upon their masters. If the master was kind, they would be contended and happy with him, and they were much better than a destitute who had a precarious living. But, if the master was bad, the lot of the slave must be woeful. In *Mṛchchhakatikam* of Śūdraka, we see that Sthavaraka was beaten and put in fetters by his cruel master, of course, he was ultimately freed by the decree of the new king who disgraced his master. But a female slave Madanikā was well treated by her cultured mistress who not only treated her as a friend and confidant but released her even to visit her lover.[14]

But these do not mean that a slave was without any hope of freedom.[15] Nārada states that a slave who saves his master from imminent danger to him becomes not only free but also gets a share of his master's property as a son.[16]

There was a definite procedure of emancipation of the slaves. If a master desired to free a slave, the latter was asked to bring a pitcher of water on his shoulder.[17] The pitcher was then broken by the master who sprinkled grain, water and flowers on the head of the slave and muttered thrice: *thou art free*. The slave was then set free with his face turned towards the east.[18]

The slave was, in fact, a subordinate member of his master's household. His maintenance was his master's responsibility, and if he died sonless, it was incumbent on the master to perform funeral and rites for the welfare of his soul. A slave could be bought, sold, given away or even mortgaged and loaned but the masters had no right over their lives of their slaves, and were not allowed to abandon them in old age, as was done in many other ancient civilizations. "A man may go short himself or stint his wife and children but never his slave who does his dirty work for him."[19] The right of the master to punish the slave was also limited. "A wife, a son, a slave, a servant or a younger brother may, when they do wrong, be beaten with a rope or a cane, but only on the back and not on the head. If a man beats them otherwise, he should be punished as thief."[20]

The *Arthaśāstra* lays down more humane regulations of slavery than do the *Smṛtis*.[21] Slaves are entitled to own and inherit property, and earn money in their spare time. The chastity of the slave-girl is to be protected. If a master rape his maid-slave, he must set her free paying proper compensation. If, however, he begets a child on the slave girl, both the child and the girl should become free. A promise by a man made in direct necessity to sell himself and his family is not a binding. Possibly these liberal regulations together with the living by the slave in the same household made, Megasthenes observed: "All the Indians are free and not one of them is slave . . . the Indians do not even use aliens as slaves and much less a countryman of their own."[22]

Indian economy was never dependent on slavery as was the case with Egypt, Sumer and the Greek and even the Roman civilizations.[23] In India, the labourers, farm workers and craftsmen were normally freemen and the *latifundia* of the Roman magnate had no counterpart in India. Rhys Davis has justly remarked: "We have nothing of such later (western) developments of slavery as rendered the Greek mines, the Roman *latifundia* or plantains of Christian slave owners scenes of misery and oppression. For the most part, the slaves (in India) were household servants and not badly treated, and their numbers seem to have been insignificant. Of course, there are numerous references in literature to slaves being badly treated by their masters but he was definitely better off in India than in most parts of ancient world; *dāsa* was a bondsman not a chattel slave."[24]

Slavery existed in India and the Indians were in the same situation with all other peoples in maintaining slavery whether of prisoners of war or of defaulting debtors and born-house slaves. But the treatment of slaves was very humane so much so that the foreign observers like the Greek ambassador Megasthenes or Chinese pilgrims like Fa-hien could not detect the existence of slavery in India.

8.2 Hired Labourer

The status of the hired labourer was below the status of slaves. These labourers may be broadly divided into following categories[25]:

1. Agricultural labourer and pastoral labourer or those who were engaged in tillage, field watching, tending and grazing cattle and for dairy production.
2. Industrial labourer or those who were employed in spinning, weaving in state factories or private organizations for industrial purpose.
3. Mercantile labourer employed by merchants to hawk wares, carry goods or serve the deck.
4. *Sira-vāhaka* or those who cultivated *Sira* lands for a share of the produce.
5. Finally, miscellaneous labourers working in the houses of rich persons. Śukra and Kauṭilya hold that hired labourer could be employed for agriculture, cattle rearing, trade and commerce or for carrying goods. Sometimes, soldiers were included in the category of hired labourers.

Various authorities prescribed different pay for the hired labourer. Nārada allowed 1/10th of the grain produced by the agricultural labourer.[26] Bṛhaspati allows 1/3rd of the crop without food[27]; Buddhist *saṁghas* provided bulls and land and 1/6th share of the produce, says I-tsing[28], the Chinese traveller. As for momentary payment, Kauṭilya provides for 1/4th *pāna*[29], Manu 1 *pāna* per month or cloth in every sixth month and one *drona* of grain every month.[30] Manu allows milk of one cow out of ten.

Labourers were liable to penalties for breach of contract and for damage caused by negligence as mentioned earlier. Strike to raise wage was declared illegal.[31]

8.3 *Viṣṭi*

The practice of levying forced labour or labour tax was prevalent in ancient India as in ancient Egypt and mediaeval Europe since the days of the Mauryas or even earlier.[32] Manu regards forced labour as a regular levy. Other lawgivers also sanction this.[33] The Gupta emperors also used to levy it and included all sorts of free labour and exceeded all limitations. According to *Agnipuraṇa*, the king was required to provide food for such workers. The artisans, manufacturers and free labourers had to pay one day's earning or work for the king once a month.[34]

Kauṭilya dwells at length on various types of *viṣṭi*. The village community had to build and maintain works of public utility such as wells, tanks, canals, roads and public buildings. Each member of the village had to contribute his share towards these. Rich persons could send their slaves for these works.[35] An officer, called *viṣṭibandhaka*, was appointed to procure such labourer.[36]

Forced contribution or labour of royal troops could be exacted as a matter of right by the king while visiting a village. The nobles and the rich were not exempted from it.[37] People were to carry loads, make roads, and render many other types of such services, mentions Kalhana. Hiuen-tsang also refers to it. In the sixth century A.D., it was imposed on smiths, chariot makers, barbers, potters and others.[38]

The employment of the forced labour occur for the first time in the *Bhāgawatpurāṇa*.[39] Three types of labourer are mentioned: (i) involuntary unpaid labour; (ii) involuntary paid labour; and (iii) labour service exacted by the users. In the later period, the practice of using forced labour in agriculture had gained more importance. Forced labour was exacted by religious institutions as well as secular landlords.[40] The temple of Tanjore was maintained by this forced labour.[41] The Palitana states that the land was donated with the right to forced labour. Most of the inscriptions referring to the forced labour, however, are from Madhya Pradesh and Kāthiawar.[42] Forced labour, however, cruel and immoral, was regarded lawful by Kauṭilya.[43] Buddhists and Jains did not raise any voice against it. Land was given as gift with right to forced labour. Besides, the villagers were liable to *Praṇaya* or *ex-gratia* payment of milk, grass, firewood and vegetables to the king and his officers visiting village.[44]

REFERENCES

1. *The Cultural Heritage*, Vol. II, p. 658.
2. *Ibid.*
3. A.L. Basham, *The Wonder that was India*, pp. 153-54.
4. *Ibid.*
5. *Ibid.*
6. *Mahābhārata*, *Virātparva*, pp. 33-60.
7. *Arthaśāstra*, III, p. 7.
8. *Manusmṛiti*, VIII, p. 415.
9. *Nārada*, V, pp. 25-28.

10. *Ibid.*, pp. 6-7.
11. S.K. Maity, *op. cit.*
12. *Nārada*, V, p. 41; *Manu*, VIII, p. 416.
13. *Ibid.*, I, p. 29; *Manu*, VIII, p. 70.
14. *Mṛichhakatikam*, II, III, VIII, X.
15. *Nārada*, V, p. 30.
16. *Yājñavalkya* II, p. 183.
17. *Nārada*, V, pp. 38-43.
18. *Ibid.*
19. A.L. Basham, *op. cit.*, p. 153.
20. *Manu*, VIII, p. 299.
21. A.L. Basham, *op. cit.*, p. 155.
22. *The Age of Imperial Unity*, p. 571.
23. A.L. Basham, *op. cit.*, p. 153.
24. *The Age of Imperial Unity*, p. 571.
25. *The Cultural Heritage*, Vol. II, p. 658.
26. *Nārada*, V, pp. 5-6.
27. *Bṛhaspati*, XVI, p. 13.
28. *The Classical Age*, p. 601.
29. *Ibid.*
30. *Manu*, VIII, p. 415.
31. *The Cultural Heritage*, Vol. II, p. 658.
32. S.K. Maity, *op. cit.*, p. 196.
33. *Manu*.
34-35. A.L. Basham, *op. cit.*, p. 1.
36. R. Choudhury, *op. cit.*
37. *Ibid.*
38. R.C. Majumdar, *op. cit.*, p. 1.
39. *Ibid.*
40. *Ibid.*
41. *Ibid.*
42. S.K. Maity, *op. cit.*, p. 198.
43. *Arthaśāstra*, II, p. 7.
44. A.L. Basham, *op. cit.*, pp. 96-97, 109.

9

CURRENCY AND CREDIT

In economics money has four functions which is well expressed in this couplet — "Money is a matter of functions four, a medium, a measure, a standard and a store."[1] The idea developed gradually, yet its function as measure, a medium, and a standard were well understood in the ancient times. During the Vedic times cattle has assumed the nature of currency. The Vedic *Āryans* prayed for the increase of cattle, warriors seized the cattle as booty, the priest received cattle as fees, and values were reckoned in terms of cattle. In this period, however, barter was the usual method of trade. From the sixth century onwards bigger transactions began to be carried on with the dust of gold measured by weight.[2] We know from Herodotus that Achaemanian emperors received 360 talent in gold dust from their Indian province as tribute.[3]

From fifth century B.C., uninscribed punch mark coins of recognized weight and fineness began to assume the medium of exchange.[4] Buddhist texts refer that *kahapāna*, gold, silver, copper and bronze coins called *kaṁsa, pada, māsaka, kakanika* were in circulation in different places. Silver punch mark coins of 5th to 4th century B.C. have been found in south Bihar and eastern Uttar Pradesh.[5] During the time of the Mauryas, they appeared in the mid of Gangā valley. The punch mark coins found in Orissa, Andhra Pradesh and western India belong to 300 B.C.[6] Some pre-Sātavāhana coins have been found in Deccan.[7] But these are uninscribed and without any portrait. Early coins were tribal and primitive in conception, have irregular shape and rude in execution.[8] But the coins of preceding and succeeding Christian era show an improvement in size and design. Thousands of metallic punch mark coins have been unearthed.[9] They have no inscription but the punch marks probably show the emblem of the kings who minted the coins and control marks of the officials and merchants from different parts of the country.[10] In the Maurya empire, the money economy was an established fact.

Major transactions were made in currency, and officials received their salary in *pāna* as well.[11]

The earlier coins were based on the weight system given in *Manu-Smṛti*[12] of which the unit was called *raktika* (ratti or *gunja* berry, *i.e.* 15/14 grains). *Suvarṇa* was the standard gold coins of 80 *ratis*, while the copper coins of the same weight was called *kārsapāna*. A copper coin of 100 ratis called *pāna* was also known. *Puraṇa* or *dharana* of 32 ratis was the silver coin.

The *Arthaśāstra* provides for state monopoly of coinage; the mint master received bullion from the public to be struck into coins on payment of seigniorage charges. But the earlier specimens show that kings, guilds and even merchants issued coins duly marked with their symbols signifying correctness of weight and purity of the metal.[13] There is a large variety of these signs or symbols, more than three hundred in number, and sometimes several of them are found on one or both sides of the coins. The Maurya tradition of issuing currency was continued by the Śakas, Pallavas and Kuṣāṇas who by and large followed the Indo-Greek standard striking similarity between the Kuṣāṇas and the Romans.[14] It is suggested that artisans of Alexandria helped both Romans and the Kuṣāṇas in minting money and that why similarity between the currencies of these two empires, even in denominations. The Kuṣāṇas, however, adjusted the eight and standard currency in their realm according to the contemporary ratio of gold and silver.[15] Some 64 coins of Wima, Kaniska, Huviska and Vasudeva have been found; these coins weigh between 118 to 123 grains of which 107 grains were pure gold.[16] This corresponds to the *Suvarṇa* standard of Manu comprising 80 *rattis* or 144 grains.[17]

The Indo-Greek issued silver coins but the Kuṣāṇas did not issue silver coins.[18] The Greek issued some gold coins but the Kuṣāṇas issued them in large numbers. In addition, the Kuṣāṇas issued plenty of copper coins, possibly following the Mauryas.[19] It is quite possible that the Kuṣāṇas had the benefit of knowledge of melting and minting from the Mauryas.[20]

The Indian system of coinage was considerably influenced by the foreign rulers who established their rules in India. For example, the Bacterian Greeks issued a series of coins with the same name and portrait of the ruler who issued them on the obverse and the figure of the deities to whom the rulers were devoted on the reverse.[21] There was also an influx of Roman coins in the Greek-Bacterian Kingdom.[22] The style of these coins greatly influenced the currency of Śaka, Pārthian, and Kuṣāṇa coinage, the form, character and standard of weight of Indian coins were changed; even foreign names like *dīnara* or *dramma* (drachma) were applied to them.[23] The fashion of issuing circular coinage bearing the superscriptions of the rulers who issued them seem to have taken firm root now. Of course, the Nanda and Maurya coins did not bear the superscriptions of the ruling kings in whose name these coins were issued. But far less rulers issued coins in their names.[24]

The legends on the coins, in the beginning, were bilingual. Greek and Indian either in *Kharosti* or *Brāhmi*.[25] Later, the coins lost the Hellenistic inspiration and were replaced by Indian or Sythoparthian; the coins as a whole, however, suffer in chastity of design and elegance in execution.[26]

Later the Kuṣāṇa ruler, Kuṣāṇa-III and Vāsudeva continued to issue gold coins resembling earlier Kuṣāṇa types.[27] On the adverse, there was king offering oblation at the altar with a legend in Greek which gradually degenerated and was replaced by *Brāhmi* script.[28] The reverse has two types — in one there is Śiva standing by his bull and on the other Ardoksha seated on the throne as on Huviska's coin which weigh 120 grains.

Sythians, successors of the Kuṣāṇas continued the tradition. The weight of these coins is same but debased. These coins are found in Central and Western Punjab. The names of the kings who issued them are written in *Brāhmi*.[29]

The Śaka Kṣatraps of Western India issued coins of established type.[30] Later the Gupta Emperor Chandragupta-II issued silver coins possibly following them. Śaka coins have bust of the king on the obverse with meaningless Greek legend which resembled the Indo-Bacterian prototype.[31] The *Brāhmi* legend on the reverse mentions the name and title of the ruler and his father. From the time Jivadaman (C 175 A.D.), coins began to bear the name of the king and the date of the coin behind the bust of the king.[32] No other king issued such a series of dated coins. The later Kuṣāṇas-Sythians issued no copper coins. A few Kṣatrap rulers issued copper coins. They were usually anonymous with elephant on the obverse and three arched hills on the reverse with the sun and moon on either side with the date of issuance below.[33]

Monetisation reached its zenith during the time of the Imperial Guptas. As many as sixteen hordes of these coins have been found so far.[34] These followed the Kuṣāṇa standard.[35] The Gupta issued gold, silver, copper and silver plated copper coins. These coins were influenced by the foreigners. But in the South, this influence is hardly noticeable.

The earlier gold coins of Guptas weigh 118 to 123 grains of which 107 grains were pure gold.[36] Later coins became heavier in weight, being 140 grains of which gold content was 70 grains, *e.g.* coins of Skandagupta.[37]

The Guptas, to start with, followed the Kuṣāṇa style and standard and gradually developed their own system. The Kuṣāṇa coins depicted the portrait of the King on the obverse and the deity of the reigning king on the reverse.[38] Goddess Nana is found seated on a lion on the coins of Huviska and Kaniska as on the coins of Chandragupta which show a goddess on the reverse.[39] The king, of course, puts on a cap instead of the Kuṣāṇa head-gear. Thus from the reign of Chandragupta-I, gold coins began to be struck and the practice continued till the reign of Viṣṇugupta. The coins of Chandragupta-I, Samudragupta and Chandragupta-II weighed 123 grains of which 107 grains was pure gold, a standard set by the Kuṣāṇas.[40] But towards the end of the reign of Skandagupta, the coins became heavier weighing an average 144 grains of which gold content was between 87 per cent to 54 per cent.[41] During the successors of Skandagupta, gold coins were issued, possibly to supply the demand of the kingdom.[42] But due to financial stringency, the gold content appreciably declined and variety was also limited. For example, Samudragupta issued not less than seven varieties of gold coins. Chandragupta-II issued two classes of archer type coins and so on.

Besides the gold coins, the Guptas issued silver coins from reign of Chandragupta-II. Chandragupta-I issued some silver currency after the conquest of western India from the Śakas who used to strike silver coins in their kingdom.[43] These coins were modelled on the satrapal coins and meant for circulation in that region. His son and successor Kumargupta-I minted silver coins of two types in plenty, possibly one meant for western India and the other for the central provinces of his empire.[44] But we find different classes of these coins of several varieties. Among the later Guptas, only Skandagupta and Buddhagupta continued the silver coinage.[45] Similar peacock variety of coins were issued by the Hunas, the Mukharíes and the Puṣyabhūti later.[46] This can be safely concluded that these coins were issued to supplement the gold currency of the Gupta kings.

The silver plated copper coins or silver coins with copper core of Kumārgupta-I and Skandagupta have raised doubts as to the genuineness of these as regular currency of that period. Smith who had studied these coins systematically regards them as real coinage and not mere forgeries of the silver coins of these kings.[47] He holds that these copper coins were issued in accordance with the precedence of Nahapāna and many other kings. He, of course, believes that these were debased silver coins issued during the financial stringency of the Gupta empire; these were in fact genuine copper coinage. Allan also thinks that these were originally silver plated coins, perhaps merely washed with silver, intended to pass as silver currency.[48]

These coins have been found in and around Valabhi and possibly intended to circulate in that region after this area was cut off from the empire by the Huna invasion.[49] In addition to the gold and silver coins, we have copper coins of Gupta period. R.D. Banerjee has referred two copper coins of Samudragupta but unfortunately those are untraced.[50] Six copper coins of problematic Rāmagupta, the type, fabric and meteorology of which correspond to the coins of Chandragupta-II from whose region large number of copper coins were issued.[51] So far nine types of copper coins of Chandragupta-II have been found and these appear to owe little to any preceding copper coinage.[52] The copper coins of his son and successor Kumārgupta-I are rare.[53] Later copper coins are not found. Possibly copper coins were not hoarded because of its cheapness and these were melted down for its mettalic use. Further copper is more liable to corrosion than gold and silver. After the fall of Guptas, the various provinces and principalities issued their coins. But they lack uniformity of design and weight and their number is surprisingly small.

It is difficult to determine the relative value of gold, silver and copper coins. The data are meagre and no fixed standard was followed for copper currency. Average value of gold and silver was 1:8 during the time of Darious, the Persian Emperor.[54] Relative value of these metals did not fluctuate much but values of silver and copper varied to a great extent. Average gold and silver coins weigh 120 and 30 grains respectively. Towards the middle of the 5th century A.D. weight of gold coins rose to 148 grains, 16 pieces of silver were equal to one gold coin.[55] Gold coins contained 50 per cent gold, a little higher than Sātavāhana coins whose gold : silver ratio was 9:1; ratio of silver and copper varied between 50:1 and 70:1. *Smṛtis* provide 16 copper *pānas* weighing 144 grains, 16 *karsapanas* weighing 16 grains. Kuṣāṇa and Gupta silver coins of 30 grains might have been equal to 16 copper.[56]

Thus, we may conclude that metallic currency had become a regular feature of the economic life of the country in the Classical period. Besides the coins of the Guptas, we have metallic coins of the Roman and Byzantine empires[57] in India in this period. Of course, regular currency was supplemented by *cowries* or conch shells for smaller transactions and carter might have been existed.

The concept of legal tender never seems to have taken note in ancient India and coins were often current beyond the borders of the kingdom which minted them. Some important dynasties such as Pālas of Bengal did not regularly mint coins but relied on those of the other states.[58]

Coins circulated less rapidly than they do now-a-days and might be current for centuries. The *Periplus of the Erythnean Sea*, a Greek text of the first Century A.D. notice that the coins of Menander, who ruled in Punjab, at least two centuries earlier, were current in the port of Barygaza (Bhṛgukachha, modern Broach) which was 500 miles away from Menānder's kingdom.[59] Foreign currency circulated freely. In the north-west, Athenian drachma, as well as local imitations were current before the invasion of Alexander and Achaemenid. Seleucid, Pārthian, Romān, Sāsānian and Islamic coins were used at different periods.[60] In the South numerous hoards of Roman coins have been found.

9.1 Credit

Though there is no evidence of a highly organized financial machinery of cheques, drafts and letters of credits, usuary or money lending at interest except by the *Brāhmaṇas* was widespread and did not incur the reprobation of the Hindu society as it did not of the mediaeval Christianity and Islam. But usuary is allowed to people of all classes in times of distress. The *Brāhmaṇas* and *Kṣtriyas*, of course, are allowed to be charged at a nominal interest.[61] Therefore, money lending was restricted to only the *Vaiśyas* and *Śūdras*. Wealth acquired by money lending was termed as "spotted wealth". Yet money lending was justified on legal, moral and economic background. Besides trade, guilds acted as bankers, both recovering deposits and issuing loans. Larger temples sometimes served as bankers and in the South the village commune occasionally made loans to peasants.[62]

There were professional users who earned their living by money lending. Usuary was a contract between the lender and the borrower and the state usually did not interfere except in extreme cases of injustice. Usually, the rules current in money lending circles and guilds were respected. Moreover, local customs were given due weight in making loan contract, fixing interest and recovery of debt.[63] Bṛhaspati declares that it is by local custom that the loan and its recovery should be regulated.[64]

Money was lent by contract in which both security and surety were necessary. Various kinds of securities were suggested by lawgivers. Bṛhaspati states that a creditor should not lend money without any pledge or adequate value or a deposit or a trustworthy security, nor without a bond written by the debtor himself.[65] A pledge could be of four kinds, *viz.* movable or immovable property to be kept only to be released at any time or limited as to time which should be stated in writing or stipulated orally before witness.[66]

A pledge was supposed to be preserved previously in the same condition as at the time of its delivery. Otherwise, the creditor could not claim interest. If a pledge was given for enjoyment then the creditor could not charge interest for he was supposed to have enjoyed interest by enjoyment.[67] Thc creditor, of course, could appropriate the pledge after the stipulated period if the loan is not discharged as contracted. When a pledge though carefully kept loses its value after a certain period, the debtor either gives another pledge or discharges the debt to the creditor.[68] On the other hand, if a pledge is destroyed or injured by the negligence of the creditor he must make the good same, provided the loss was caused by fate or the King.[69] A pledge for custody must not be issued, unless its specific use is mentioned clearly in the agreement. If the creditor does so, he should not demand interest from the debtor.[70] Further he must make good the pledge to the debtor. Otherwise, he is considered as a thief.[71]

When a field or an immovable property has been enjoyed and more than the principal amount is realized by it, the debtor shall recover the pledge automatically; and when the principal has been realized together with interest, the creditor, should restore the field or property to the debtor.[72] Bṛhaspati further stipulates that when the principal has been doubled or the stipulated period expired in the case of pledge delivered for a certain time only — the creditor becomes the owner of the pledge, after waiting for a fortnight.[73] Further when the amount of debt is doubled by the interest accruing to it, and the debtor is either dead or no longer present, the creditor may take his cattle and sell it before witnesses.[74]

Another fruitful instrument in the hand of the creditor was surety.[75] Sureties were responsible for four purposes, namely for appearance, for confidence, for payment and for delivering the assets of the debtor, who may abscond. He vouches for the honesty of the debtor to the effect that he will pay the debt.[76] Thirdly, the surety undertakes to pay the debt himself together with interest should the debtor fail to pay.[77] And finally the surety is under the obligation to deliver his movable property, such as household furniture in the same case.[78] The sureties of the first two types are under obligation to pay the debt of the debtor in due times, but their sons were under no obligation to pay for the debtors.[79] If the sureties of the last two types fail to pay themselves the debt, their sons are held responsible for the payment.[80] But, the sureties are to pay in installments and should not be pressed for payment when the debtor is present.[81] In case of plurality of the sureties, the debt should be shared proportionately according to the agreement.[82] But, if they are bound severely, the payment shall be made by any of them as the creditor pleases.[83]

The loans whether secured or unsecured had to be executed by a written document and every part of payment made by the debtor should be discharged by a receipt. If the creditor does not give a receipt although being asked for it, the creditor shall lose the remainder of the sum due to him.[84] Though Megasthenes writes that Indians do not have written laws, for the Classical period, written document for the credit had to be executed properly.[85]

Nārada and Bṛhaspati lay down validity and utility of documents. A document has to be shown on every occasion to meetings of families, associations of traders, assemblies of cohabitants and other bodies of persons and read it out to them and remind them by it in order to establish its validity.[86] Further a document remains valid if the demand recorded in it has been repeatedly urged and publicly proclaimed, even after the death of the witness.[87] If a document is transferred to another country, or burnt, or written badly or stolen, a delay may be granted, in case it exists.[88] But, if it is lost, the evidence of those who have seen it shall be final.[89] If a document is spoilt or torn, stolen, defaced, lost or badly written, another document has to be executed, should, however, a doubt subsist as to whether a document is authentic, or fabricated, its validity should be established by examining the writing of the party, the name of the subscribing witness of the document, the marks and circumstantial evidence, and probabilities of the case.[90]

A writing which has been neither seen nor read for thirty years should be invalid even though subscribing witness be living.[91] A bond ceases to be valid if the witness, creditor, debtor and the scribe be dead, unless its validity can be established by the existence of a pledge.[92] Further if document is neither heard of becomes invalid even though the witness be living.[93] If the witness of the deed is infamous or reproached by the people, the document is called a false one.[94] Lastly, a document spoiled by fire, or executed long ago or soiled with dirt, or intended for a very short period, or containing a number of mutilated or effaced syllabus, is reckoned as a false document.[95]

9.2 Interest

Natural rate of interest laid down by *Smṛti* was 1.25 per cent. But 2 per cent from the priestly class, 3 per cent from military class, 4 per cent from trading and industrial class and 5 per cent from agricultural and labouring class was also prescribed.[96] Possibly the latter rate was for unsecured loans.

Six kinds of interest are mentioned in the legal texts.[97] They are:

1. *Kayika* or bodily, so called because of the pledge could be used by the creditor, *e.g.* the milk of a cow or beast of burden to be engaged by the creditor;
2. *Kalika* or periodical, due at a stipulated time;[98]
3. *Chakravṛdhhi* or compound interest;[99]
4. *Karita* or stipulated interest (it might be over and above normal rate of interest); [100]
5. *Śikhavṛdhhi* or interest to be drawn everyday till the principal is paid;[101] and
6. *Bhogalābha* or interest drawn by enjoyment, such as enjoyment of products of a field or use of a house kept in pledge.[102]

Bṛhaspati states that hair-interest, bodily interest and interest by enjoyment should be taken till the principal is unpaid.[103]

There are cases where no interest can be charged. Interest on short term loans cannot be charged from a friend unless there is an agreement for the purpose; of course interest accrues on such a loan after 1/2 year.[104] Nārada states that loan given to a friend does not yield interest unless the creditor asks refund. If the friend does not pay the loan then interest of 5 per cent should be charged by the creditor.[105]

Gautama and Manu state that interest can grow only upto the sum equal to the principal, after which it ceases to accumulate.[106] But later, Nārada prescribes that loan can grow to thrice to four times, liquids octuple, interest of women and cattle may grow up to one issue.[107] Bṛhaspati holds that gold grow twice, clothes and base metals to thrice, grain, edible plants, cattle and wool to four times, and salt, oil and spirit to eight times.[108]

Then if a debtor was prevented by misfortune to repay the debt he was to pay gradually according to his means. But, if a wealthy debtor refuses to pay out of malice, the king could compel him to pay and charge 5 per cent for himself.[109]

A debt unlimited by time is passed on to sons, grandsons, lawful heirs or joint partners of the debt. The son of a debtor was under obligation to discharge the loan of his father, if his father died before he could repay the debt.[110] The loan of the paternal grandfather had to be paid before the above two.[111] The debt was not carried on to the fourth generation.

There was joint leading business. In such cases, the interest was to be shared proportionately. If any partner failed to join other partners, the defaulting partner should receive no interest.[112] Those who lend jointly gold grain, liquids and condiments, or like, the gain should be equal to their shares. Nārada states that in partnership, every partner is liable to the business debts contracted by any partner.[113] But the son of one partner is not bound to pay the loan of the partner.[114, 115]

Non-payment of debt was supposed to incur a sin which had to be atoned in future life. It was believed if a man died without paying the debt, he would be born again in the house of the creditor as a slave to repay the debt by his labour.[116] If an ascetic or Agnihotri died without discharging the debt, the entire merit of these persons go to the creditor.[117] These notions provided incentive to clear off the debt by the debtor in his life time.

9.3 Recovery of Debt

If a debtor denies his debt, the creditor first should try to convince the debtor by citing the place, the contents of the written documents and so forth by means of argument.[118] But when persuasions, an ordeal must be administered by fire, water, proof of virtues and so forth, which was appropriate to the place, to the season and to strength of the debtor.[119]

Bṛhaspati and Nārada have given much lattitude to creditor for the realization of debt. They prescribe that by gentle persuasion, fraud, force or legal proceedings a creditor can realize his money from the debtor.[120] Bṛhaspati further goes to say that the creditor may take the debtor to his house and compel him to pay the amount by beating or by other forcible means.[121] Moreover, he may confine his wife, son or cattle, or he may compel the debtor to do all kinds of work at his house.[122] The king shall not stand on the way. But this method does not apply to the *Brāhamaṇas* who are to pay gradually.[123] If the debtor acknowledge his debt in the court, the king was to realize 10 per cent as a fine and twice as much if the debtor was convicted after denial of the debt.[124]

It is found that the earlier *Smṛtis* did not lay down elaborate rules and regulations for money lending and expounded interest rate which recognized the said system of *varṇa* and predominance of the *Brāhmaṇs*. Possibly credit was not given due to importance to encourage trade and industry as the *Āryans* were still under influence of agro-pastoral economy. But from 600 B.C. onwards, as trade and commerce developed as a result of growth in agricultural and industrial output credit was necessary and elaborate rules and regulations were drawn up for credit. The pre-eminences of the custodians of the society, however, was maintained as we find the *Brāhmaṇas* enjoying the special facilities in discharging their debts. On the other hand, traders and producers had to pay higher interest and thus productivity suffered and commerce discouraged to borrow. The debtors were practically at the mercy of the creditors and this vicious system seems to have persisted through centuries to the modern times when it is aptly told that the "*Indian peasants are born in debts, live in debts and die in debts.*"

REFERENCES

1. S.N. Sen and S.K. Das, *An Introduction to Economic Theory*, Calcutta, 1952, p. 322.
2-3. *The Age of Imperial Unity*, p. 607.
4. A.L. Basham, *op. cit.*, p. 212.
5. *The Age of Imperial Unity*, p. 607.
6. *Ibid.*
7-11. *Ibid.*, pp. 534-608.
12. *The Cultural Heritage*, Vol. II, p. 664.
13. *Ibid.*, p. 663.
14-17. R. Choudhury, *op. cit.*, pp. 236-39.
18. R.S. Sharma, *op. cit.*, pp. 184-92.
19-26. *The Age of Imperial Unity*, pp. 585-608.
27-35. *The Vākataka-Gupta Age*, p. 295.
36-37. S.K. Maity, *op. cit.*, pp. 215-17.
38-40. *The Vākataka-Gupta Age*, p. 295.
41-42. S.K. Maity, *op. cit.*, p. 217.
43-45. *Ibid.*, pp. 217-19.
46. *The Vākataka-Gupta Age*, p. 295.
47-53. *Ibid.*, pp. 215-16.
54-56. *Ibid.*, p. 295.
57-62. A.L. Basham, *op. cit.*, p. 223.
63-64. *Bṛhaspati*, VIII, p. 24.
65-68. *Bṛhaspati*, X, pp. 6-48.

69. *Ibid.*, p. 126.
70-74. *Bṛhaspati*, X, pp. 51-67.
75. *Ibid.*, p. 73.
76. *Nārada* I, p. 148.
77. *Bṛhaspati*, X, p. 74.
78-83. *Ibid.*
84. S.K. Maity, *op. cit.*, p. 233.
85. *Ibid.*, p. 234.
86. *Ibid.*, p. 233.
87. *Nārada* I, p. 141.
88. *Bṛhaspati*, VI, p. 32.
89-95. S.K. Maity, *op. cit.*, p. 233.
96. *Ibid.*, pp. 234-35.
97. *Bṛhaspati*, X, p. 10.
98. *Nārada* I, p. 103.
99. *Bṛhaspati*, X, p. 9.
100. *Ibid.*, X, pp. 13-14.
101. *Ibid.*, X, p. 9.
102-103. *Ibid.*
104-105. *Nārada* I, p. 108.
106. *Gautama*, XIII, p. 30; *Manu* VIII, p. 151.
107. *Nārada* I, p. 106.
108. *Bṛhaspati*, X, pp. 17-18.
109. *Nārada* I, pp. 13-32.
110. *Ibid.*, I, pp. 2-4.
111. *Bṛhaspati*, X, pp. 13-14.
112. *Bṛhaspati*, XIII, p. 25.
113. *Bṛhaspati*, XIV, p. 4.
114. *Nārada* I, p. 15.
115-117. *Ibid.*, pp. 7-15.
118-119. *Ibid.*, pp. 238-39.
120-122. *Bṛhaspati*, X, pp. 90-91.
123. *Nārada* I, p. 123.
124. *Bṛhaspati*, X, pp. 904-05.

10

REVENUE AND EXPENDITURE

Ancient Indian authorities of state craft stress the need for a full-fledged treasury and provided for a regular system of taxation. The importance of the state treasury is evident from the fact that *koṣa* (treasury) was considered to be one of the seven constituent elements of the state; it was of supreme importance along with the army. The prime necessity of a competent army and a rich treasury for subduing the subversive elements on the king's side as well as those in the opposite camp for the well-being of the state was constantly emphasized by the *Arthaśāstra*[1], the *Mahabhārata*[2], *Kāmandakiya Nītisāra*[3] and *Viṣṇudharmottara Purāṇa*.[4] This is quite understandable when one considers the unstable political conditions of the time demanding constant preparedness for war because of the constant danger from the neighbouring states.[5] Further provision had to be made against feminines, not a phenomenon of rare occurrence.[6] In ancient times, when state loans were unknown, the only means available for a state to tide over a crisis was the possession of a well-stocked treasury and granary.[7] Richness of the treasury depended upon the surplus of revenue over expenditure, and therefore, elaborate rules were laid down for the efficient accounting of public receipts and expenditure and their auditing. Śukra emphasizes the keeping of daily, monthly and annual accounts, and entering of several items of income on the left side of accounts and those of the expenditure on the right side. Somadeva recommends the appointment of auditors when there is discrepancy in the items of income and expenditure.

Various sources of revenue are enumerated in legal texts as well as *Arthaśāstra*. Kauṭilya classifies the sources or items of revenue differently at different places.[8] Two important classifications are, however, *Āyasarira* (body of income) and *Āyamukha* (source of income), each being subdivided under seven heads. *Āyasarira*, which refers to the convenient centres of collection, comprises *durga* (fortified cities), *rāstia* (rural areas), *khani* (mines), *setu* (irrigation works), *vana* (forests), *varaja* (herds) and *vāripatha* (river-borne trade routes). *Bhāga* (royal share), *vyāji* (compensation), *parigha* (gate duty), *kipṭa* (fixed tax), *rupaka* (premia on coins) and *atyaya* (money fine) are the subdivisions of *Āyamukha*.

Another classification is *anyajata* (accidental revenue), *vartamāna* (current revenue) and *payusita* (outstanding revenue), Kāmandaka enumerates eight principal categories (*astavarga*) of filling the treasury through the heads of the departments[9], *viz.* agriculture, trade routes (both land and water), the capital, the water-embankments, catching of the elephants, working mines, collecting gold etc., levying wealth (from the rich) and founding towns and villages in inhabited traces. It will be seen that these classifications do not differentiate between direct and indirect taxes, rents, fees, royalties and non-tax receipts.

The principal source of revenue, however, was taxation. In the financial theories of the *Arthaśāstra* and allied works, the ruler's right to levy taxes and contributions and the people's obligation to pay them from an implied contract between the state and its subjects.[10] The imposition of taxes depends solely on the protection afforded by the State. The principles that guided the state in matters of taxation show the solicitude of the economists for the welfare of the community. Taxation was to be reasonable and equitable; the criterion of judging its equitableness consisted in the feeling of the state in one hand and that of agriculturists and the traders on the other, that they received adequate and reasonable return for their mutual services.[11] The first principle was that, in matters of taxation, the state was to be guided by the rules in the *Smṛitis*.[12] The tax was to be collected at a specified time and place and at a definite proportion or percentage. Any increase in taxation, if unavoidable, was to be gradual.[13] Additional taxation was an exceptional measure to be resorted to only under grave national emergency in the absence of any other alternative.[14] An article was to be taxed only once. Net profit, and net gross earning, was the basis for taxation of trade and industry.[15]

In the context of the canons of taxation, it is worthwhile to note whether there were any limit to the king's levying exorbitant taxes. Kauṭilya has considered the point, and according to him, the treat of disaffection among his subjects and their possible migration to another country appears to have worked as deterrent on the kings taxing their subjects beyond their means.[16] In a similar vein, the *Mahābhārata* states that *Vaiśyas*, if neglected, would disappear from the kingdom and would reside in the forest.[17] *Yājñavalkya*[18] points out that the king who extracts taxes by unjust means not only loses his wealth, but also goes to destruction along with his relatives.

10.1 Land Revenue

From the numerous references in our epigraphic records, we see that the land revenue formed the greatest sources of wealth to the royal treasury. Generally speaking, the state claimed one-sixth of the produce of the land from the people in return for the protection given to their persons and property. The principle of the payment of the 'sixth' was so strongly entrenched on the thought of the people that Kālīdāsa states that by protecting ascetics from obstacles and wealth from robber, the king was entitled to one-sixth of the religious merits of the *Aśramas*.[19] This is called the subsistence allowance (*Vṛttih*) of the king. Even the hermits in the penance grove were not free from taxation; and it is said that the sixth part of the rice collected by these ascetics was placed on the bank of the river to be taken away by the royal officers. But the king Duśyanta, instead of accepting any revenue from the saints accepted only one-sixth of the merit of their religious observances (*Tapasyā*).[20] The account of Kālīdāsa is fully corroborated by Nārada, who states that one-sixth of the produce of the soil forms the royal revenue.[21] It is taken as the reward of the king for the protection of his subjects.

This is also supported by the earlier lawgivers, with certain variations in taxation. Manu states that a king should receive from his subjects a sixth, eighth or twelfth parts of the crops, possibly according to the fertility of the soil.[22] But the *Śukranīti* of the later period is more severe and recommends a realization of one-third, one-fourth or one-half from places which are irrigated by tanks, canals and wells, by rains and rivers respectively.[23] He advocates one-sixth only from the barren land.[24]

Thus one-sixth was, according to our lawgivers, the customary share of the king from the product of the soil. We have very insignificant evidences of this in Gupta times, and we must, therefore, assume that tax was in the form of a proportion of actual crop. No Gupta inscription directly states the proportion demanded in practice, but from the Baigram and Paharpur copper plates, which give the king one-sixth of the religious merit accruing from a donation, we may assume that this proportion was the standard rate in this period too, though, as at most other times, it might often have been exceeded.[25] Besides this, there were various other taxes and royal dues, such as *udranga*, *uprikara*, *kipta*, *upkipta*, *hiraṇya*, *bāli* and the supply of forced labour (*viṣṭi*) and dairy products.[26]

Direct evidence of taxation is rather scanty in epigraphs. But from the references to the exemption from various kinds of royal dues, to their transference to the donee, or to the granting of certain taxes while others were kept reserved by the donor himself, we can trace an outline picture of revenue system of this period.

Among the commonest revenue terms, we find *bhāga-bhogakara* in the inscriptions.[27] *Kara* is often used to indicate tax in general, and in this sense it will be examined later on.[28] Fleet suggests that the term *bhāga-bhoga* may perhaps be considered as one fiscal expression indicating "enjoyment of taxes", though its literal meaning is "enjoyment of shares."[29] Sometimes, the two words are used in reverse order and are recorded as *bhoga-bhāga*.[30] If we agree with Fleet that *bhāga-bhoga* is one word, then *bhoga-bhāga* is also a single word; and its meaning is as suggested by him "share of enjoyment."[31] But these terms are used separately in some early sources. D.C. Sircar explains *bhāga* as the royal share of the produce and *bhoga* as the periodical supplies of fruits, firewood, flowers etc., which the villagers had to furnish to the kings.[32]

A.N. Bose suggests that: "There are two taxes, one the regular *bhāga*, and the other is the irregular *bāli* which is fixed at 1/4."[33] The *Arthaśāstra* also mentions *bhāga* with *bāli*, *kara* etc. under the title *rāṣtra*, which includes the tax one-sixth (*sadbhāga*) with *bāli* and *kara* etc. under the same general heading.[34] In this case *bhāga* undoubtedly means the king's customary share of the produce, normally, though not universally, amounting to one-sixth. Bhattasvāmin commenting on this, explains *sadbhāga* in general sense of the royal share (*rāja-bhāga*).[35] He further adds that the term one-sixth includes by implication other shares such as one-third and one-fourth prevailing in different tracts. Besides this, "*bhāga* seems to have been applied in the *Arthaśāstra* only as a natural extension of meaning other taxes of a similar nature."[36] We have thus in *Arthaśāstra* the term *udakabhāga*, meaning the water tax paid by the cultivators of wet lands at varying rates.[37] Another example of the *bhāga* occurs in the *Arthaśāstra* where we have the term *lavanabhāga*, meaning the king's share of the salt which is levied from manufacturers, probably working under state licences.[38]

The *bhoga* of the inscriptions[39] and of Manu[40] probably means daily presents in the form of flowers, fruits, vegetables, grasses etc., for it is interpreted by Medhatithi and Kulluka as such.[41] The custom of giving presents to the king on special occasions was very common in ancient India. When Aja started for his marriage, on the way he received clothes, grains and various other kinds of presents from the village people.[42] Sometimes, cow herds are described as visiting the king on tour, with gifts of freshly-made *ghee*. Thus *bhoga* may be the right of enjoying the abundance of flowers, milk, hide, charcoal etc. as referred to in the inscriptions.

Sometimes, the state also demanded forced labour (*viṣṭi*). Moreover, "services in labour and gifts of provisions were expected by the king and his officer when on tour, and might put small rural communities in serious difficulties."[43] As, for instance, three merchant brothers were returning from the port of Tāmralipti to their home to Ayodhyā with a caravan of merchandise and provisions. They rested for the night at a village. Meanwhile, the local king Ādisiṁha was passing by on a hunting expedition with a large band of followers and demanded provisions from the villagers. But, they were suffering from a temporary shortage and could not meet this demand. So they sent a deputation to the merchants who at their request gave the king provisions from their own stock.[44]

The *kara* is another form of revenue frequently mentioned in the epigraphs.[45] This fiscal term was apparently unknown in the early Vedic literature. However, in the *Dharmaśāstra, kara* is common designation of the land tax. But the *Arthaśāstra*[46] and Manu[47] give a rather difficult explanation. The significance of *kara* in the Manu is differently interpreted by different commentators. It is shown by the following examples as gifts of commodities (*eravyadinam-Medhatithi*), a fixed gold payment on land (*bhuminiyatam devan hiraṇyam-Sarvajna paraṇaya*), contribution in the form of grass, wood etc. (*gulmadayad ikam Rāmachandra*), contribution from villagers and townsmen either monthly or at *Bhādrapada* and *Paus* (*gramapuravasibhya pratimasam bhadrapause-niyamena grahyan* — Kulluka), a monthly payment by villagers (*gramavasibhya pratimasikam* — Rāghavānanda). The last two interpretations are very much in agreement with Bhattasvamin's explanation of the term in his commentary on the *Arthaśāstra*.[48]

The *kara* thus appears to be of the nature of periodical tax levied more or less universally on the villagers. It is apparently this vague and unsatisfactory definition that has led modern interpreters of the *Arthaṣāstra* to attempt to find a more suitable meaning. Thus, in connection with the above passage, Dr. Shama Shastry translates it in one place as "tax paid in money", and in another place as "taxes on subsidies that are paid by vassal kings and others."[49] In his German translation of *Arthaśāstra*, Meyer[50], while rendering it on the authority of Bhattasvāmin as annual tax (*Fahressteur*), thinks Shastry's first explanation to be possibly correct. He also at the same time suggests, as possible meaning, ground-tax (*Bodensteuer*). Of all these explanations, it can be said that they are not supported by any other independent evidence.

The Junagarh rock inscription of the Mahākṣatrapa Rudradamana dated CAD 150, shows *kara* in use as distinct sources of revenue at this period and throws some light upon its nature. It is said that Rudradamana met the expenses of the constructions of the dam of the Sudarśana lake out of his own treasury without oppressing his subjects by means of *kara*, *viṣṭi* and *paraṇaya*.[51] From this, it would seem that *kara* was though like *viṣṭi* (forced labour) and *praṇaya* (emergency levy) to be oppressive tax. Sircar also suggests that it was a tax to be paid besides the grain share. It would thus appear that *kara* was not a part of the regular land-tax, but a special tax which might be remitted by conscientious kings.

Another fiscal due, *bāli*, occurs in many inscriptions[52] and in literature.[53] It is the oldest Indo-Aryan term for the royal revenue. In the Ṛgveda, it is the king's share both from his subjects and from conquered kings.[54] Zimmer[55] affirms that *bāli* in the former sense was originally a voluntary offering on the part of subjects, and that only in the later times did it assume the character of a compulsory payment of tax. MacDonell and Keith[56], on the other hand, do not share the view of Zimmer. It was possible that *bāli* was from the first of the nature of a customary contributions payable by the subjects, and did not depend upon their free choice. In the Brahmanical period, *bāli* had certainly assumed the character of a tax. It is hardly likely that even a kingdom of the primitive semi-tribal type could subsist on purely voluntary contributions.[57]

In later times, when other items of taxation appear along with *bāli*, it is only used in a special sense. Sometimes in the *Jātakas*[58], *bāli* is used in the sense of additional and oppressive taxes. In the Milindapānho[59], *bāli* is mentioned as an emergency tax from which the four chief ministers were free. Moreover, in the Rummidei pillar inscription of Aśoka[60], it is used exclusively in the narrower sense. Dr. F.W. Thomas takes the term *ubālike* as "free from *bāli*" and rightly interprets it as a religious cess, although Hultzsch explains it more freely as "free of taxes."[61]

Accepting Thomas' definition of *bāli*, we can translate *ubālike* as "free from religious cess." The significance of the whole passage then would be that, the village, in consideration of its being the birth-place of

Load Buddha, had its rate of land revenue reduced by Aśoka to the one-eighth, while the additional cess was abolished altogether.[62] This interpretation of *bāli* as a religious tax of some kind is quite in agreement without epigraphic records, for in our period, whenever the term *bāli* occurs, it is recorded along with *charu* and *sattra*. The *bāli* like *charu* is an offering to the gods, comprising clarified butter, grain, rice, fruits, flowers and so on. Even today, Indian villages in common religious festivals offer these to the gods by collecting general contributions, and in that sense, *bāli* can be explained as a sort of religious cess or a contribution to the state.[63]

Another fiscal term *uparikara* sometimes occur in the inscriptions. Fleet suggests that it is derived from the word '*upari*' or '*upri*' at first, and interpretes it as "a tax levied on the cultivators who had no proprietary right in the soil."[64] But in all these inscriptions, the term *uparikara* is recorded along with another fiscal term *udraṅga*. This has tempted Ghoshal to conjecture that two fiscal terms have been antithetically.[65] He thus explains *udraṅga* as a tax levied on the permanent tenants and *uprikara* as a tax imposed on the temporary tenants. He connects *uparikara* with the Marathi word '*upri*', which means "a cultivator not belonging originally to a village, but residing and occupying land in it, either upon a lease for the stipulated term of years, or at the pleasure of the proprietor." The evidence for it is very tenuous, since the Mārāthi language did not develop for some ten centuries after the date of the inscription, and it is fairly rash to draw conclusions from such feeble linguistic evidence. The same contention is applicable to Ghoshal altogether as he suggests that *uparikara* is something like "the Tamil *mel-varam*, i.e. the crown's share of produce (Tamil *mel*=skt. upari)." But this term often occurs together with others such as *udraṅga* and *bhāga* which more probably imply the standard royal share, and therefore, this interpretation is improbable.[66]

It is difficult to say anything conclusively. However, in Sanskrit, Bengali and Hindi, the term '*upri*' or 'extra'. This has led D.C. Sircar to explain it as an 'extra-cess' which seems to be the most probable interpretation.[67]

The meaning of another revenue term *udaraṅga* which is referred to, is highly conjectural. According to *Sāsvatakoṣa*, it is explained by *udhāra* and *udgrantha*.[68] Following this source, Fleet explains the term as "the share of the produce collected usually for the king."[69] This is unlikely, for if *bhāga* means the regular land tax, as is generally believed, since in many inscriptions *bhāga* and *udraṅga* occur together, they imply different taxes.[70]

Ghosal interprets *udaraṅga* as a tax levied on permanent tenants in distinction to *uprikara* which, as we have seen, he interprets as a tax on temporary cultivations.[71] D.C. Sircar also holds the same opinion.[72] To strengthen his arguments Sircar further cites the Mārāthi word *udhār-jamābandi* which is an assessment of the total revenue of a village upon the proprietor, who is entitled to distribute the proportions among the peasants. Two other suggestions can be offered for the plausible explanation of those fiscal term. It is the same as *dranga*, which according to the *Rājatarangini* is a watch station. It can be taken as a sort of police tax levied on the district for the maintenance of the local police station.[73] It might also be suggested that it is an anomalous derivative of the Sanskrit word '*udhaka*' and thus it may be a water-tax. But Ghoshal's suggestion is not convincing here, for in every case *udraṅga* is recorded along with the other normal dues of the king. It, therefore, seems to be an extra imposition, whatever its nature may be, upon all kinds of tenants.

Hiraṇya is another term recorded in some of our inscriptions.[74] *Dhānya* (paddy or grain share) is recorded in the Māliya copper plate of Dharasena-II.[75] The later is apparently a royal share of certain crops paid in kind. On this analogy, Sircar explains the term *hiraṇya* as a king's share of certain crops paid in cash.[76] From its literal sense, it is a tax payable in gold or gold coins. But, it is highly unlikely that ordinary peasants paid taxes in gold among other heavy impositions, for the value of the gold coin at that time was very high. So, it is better to accept Sircar's suggestion that *hiraṇya* has in this context the conventional sense of "cash."[77]

Another fiscal term, *vāta-bhaūta* is found in Maliya copper plate of Dharasena-II.[78] But, it is recorded in the Alina copper plate of Śilāditya-VII in the reverse of *bhūta-vāta*.[79] Fleet explains that *vāta* is derived either from *vā* 'to blow' or from *vāi* 'to become dried or withered'[80], while *bhūta* is past participle of '*bhū*', which means 'to become'. But he does not elucidate the term any further. Ghoshal, on the other hand, translates it as "revenue derived from the elements and the wind."[81] It is possible that these two terms should be taken separately as different kinds of cess for the maintenance of rites respectively for the winds (*vāta*) and for the spirits (*bhūta*), in the same manner as *bāli* and *cāru*.[82]

Even today in Indian villages, to avert natural calamities due to rain and wind, the villagers worship Indra (the god of rain) and Varuna (now-a-days looked on as the god of water). Thus rites to appease the wind and rain were though essential in the agricultural life of the day. This practice was traditionally followed by the village people even in the early part of twentieth century. Probably some kind of general contributions was collected for these ceremonies either in cash or in kind.[83]

In the Khoh copper plate of Sarvanātha, the term *hālirākara* is recorded. Ghoshal suggests that this was a plough-tax.[84] It might also be an extra tax imposed on the area which could be cultivated by one plough in a single season, though any interpretation is uncertain. The *bali* as a measure of land seems hardly the likely object of a special tax. There is evidence that a later time, a land was sometimes taxed according to area, but we know that plough taxes were levied even in the Mughal times.

In the Gupta period, the king sometimes exacted dues in the form of temporarily taking cows, presumably for milk and bullocks for the cultivation of the royal lands and for drawing the state-carts.[85] But, they were generally supplied to officers on tour in a village, as is seen in the later period. They were not, however, demands for animal sacrifice, for by this time, cow had become a sacred animal.

Sometimes, in donations of land, the entrance of *cāṭas* and *bhātas* was prohibited.[86] Fleet, following the interpretation of Bühler, explains them as regular or irregular troops.[87] Dr. Bhagwanlal Indraji takes *cāṭas-bhāta* as meaning soldiers against robbers and as denoting the royal police.[88]

But from later inscriptions, we can suggest their interpretations in a more definite way. The Surat plate of Vyāghrasena makes it clear that the *cāṭas* and *bhāṭas* acted partly as police and partly as military.[89] They were appointed to arrest robbers and persons guilty of high treason. The Talcher grant of *Kulastambha* mention them along with the government employers and grant-holders and remarks that they always try to please the *rājans*.[90] Bāna also in many places mentioned *cāṭas-bhātas* together in one compound word, like the *cāṭas-bhātas* of the land grants[91] according to their cruelty and greed. In one place he describes them as talking and laughing with the slaves and servants of the nobles after taking plenty of grain from the fields. In another place, he writes that the poor were grumbling at the cruelty and ill-treatment received at their ends.

It appears, therefore, from the above references that *caṭas* and *bhatas* were persons employed for watch and ward, for collecting revenue and for arresting thieves and robbers. Probably they were in habit of collecting oppressive extra impositions and were very unpopular among the people. Perhaps they would often levy illegal taxes for their own benefit, as later, the Mārāthas levied *chauth*, and hence the right to claim freedom from their exaction was much valued by the recipients of the land-grants.[92]

Revenue from cities, trade and industry falling broadly under "fortified city" (*durga*) and "country part" (*rāṣtra*) constituted another item, including house-taxes. Tolls were levied at the city gate on a varying and valorem tariff on incoming merchandise. *Arthaśāstra* suggests that essential goods such as grain, oil, sugar, pots and cheap textiles should be taxed at one-twentieth of their value and other goods at rates varying from one-fifteenth to one-fifth. It also mentions that merchants travelling from place to place paid small road tolls for the upkeep of the road and safety.[93]

There were also profession tax, property tax, income from slaughter houses, liquor and gambling, licence fees on weights, measures and tools, customs, port dues and transit duties, fee from passport, contributions from artisans in cash or service, dues collected from *Bhairikas*, charge of one-fifth of the interest earned by money-lenders analogous to modern income-tax, shop tax which is not mentioned in the *Smṛitis* but referred to the inscriptions[94] and ten per cent sale tax as mentioned by Megasthenes.

Income from state monopolies, state establishments etc. provided another source, and these comprised mines and minerals, salt, saffron, mint, workshops, state manufactories, jail industries and elephants.[95]

Under miscellaneous and special taxes and revenues came fine from law courts, forced labour, income unclaimed, lost or owner-less property, cheat, treasury trove, occasional taxes such as those paid on the birth of a prince and irregular receipts from plunder, tribute from foundatories etc.[96] Taxes which pilgrims had to pay, such as, those levied by Chālukya Siddharāja (A.D. 1094-c. 1143) of Gujarāt from the visitors of Somnatha, or that collected at Gaya from Kasmirians performing *srāddha* (offering to the dead) there, or the pilgrim taxes collected from the Jains which Kumarapāla (c. A.D. 1145-71) of Gujarat is stated to have abolished, come under special taxes; taxes that levied from *Upanayana* (sacred thread ceremony), marriage, Vedic sacrifices, and the like also fall under the same category. Another variety of tax levied are the *Turuska-daṅda* and *Mala-daṅda* which were raised to meet the expenses necessitated by the invasions of the Turks and Mallas respectively.[97] The Chola King Virarājendra (A.D. 1063-70) supplied a later instance of levying a special tax to finance his war against the Chālukyas of Veṅgi.[98]

Emergency revenue formed yet another source. Sources of raising emergency revenue were to be tapped only under exceptional circumstances when the treasury is empty, and there was threat of impending danger. Beside benevolences, forcible loans and donations, emergency taxes, arbitrary enhancement of normal rates and fraudulent and forcible collections were made under several protests which are exhaustively dealt with the Kauṭilya and others.[99] Reference may also be made to the sale of divine images by the Mauryas, recorded by Patañjali, which must have been instrumental in filling the state treasury to a great extent.[100] It may, however, be observed that Kauṭilya prescribes that some of these taxing devices should be levied on the seditious and irreligious only and not on all.[101]

On a careful examination of grounds of partial or total remission of taxation, it is found that religious beliefs as well as humanitarian ideas of the age were responsible for exempting from taxing several classes of people like learned Brāhamaṇas and Bhikṣus. The dumb, the deaf, the blind, students studying in *Gurukulas* and heremits were also not taxable, infants, those far advanced in age, women newly confined or destitute, poor widows, and people otherwise helpless are also tax-free.[102] In view of the fact that certain villages supplied recruits to the state army, those military villages were exempted from taxations.[103] Untaxable property should including articles worth less than a copper coin[104], only a nominal tax was to be collected for the first four or five years from the agriculturists who newly brought the land under cultivation and made it more fertile and productive; but tax in their cases gradually rose to the normal rate in subsequent years.[105]

10.2 Expenditure

Although we know a lot about the state revenue, a very little is known about state expenditure. We learn from Śukra that one-sixth of the income should go to the savings, one-half should be spent on the army, one-twelfth each on charity, ministers, inferior officials, and the privy purse.[106] The *Mānasollāsa* recommends that ordinarily three-fourth of the revenue should be spent and one-fourth should be saved.[107] The observations of Megasthenes and Kauṭilya's regulations indicate that the head of national defence absorbed a considerable portion of the revenue, the other items on expenditure side answered the obligations of a welfare state including the King's privy purse, civil list for the King and the court, his ministers and officers, police and other protective establishments etc.[108]

It seems, therefore, that much of the income of the state was stored and the effect of the doctrine was bad. The great reverse of the precious metals and jewels, not touched except dire emergency, were economically useless and the cause of greed of other kingdoms and this is an important factor of foreign invasions which ultimately destroyed Hindu India, as aptly pointed out by Prof. A.L. Basham.[109]

REFERENCES

1. *Arthaṣāstra* II, p. 8.
2. *Mahābhārata*, XII, 119.16.
3. *Kāmandaka*, XIII, 33.
4. *Viṣnupurāṇa*, II, 61.17.
5-7. *The Cultural Heritage*, Vol. II, p. 665.
8. *Kauṭilya*, VII.5.
9. *Kāmandaka*.
10-15. *The Cultural Heritage*, Vol. II, pp. 666-67; A.L. Basham, *op. cit.*, p. 110.
16. *Kauṭilya*, VII.5.
17. *Mahābhārata*, XII, 87.36.
18. *Yājñavalkya* 1.3.10.
19. *Raghuvaṁsa*, XVII, p. 65.
20. *Śakuntala*, V, p. 850.
21. *Nārada*, XVIII, p. 48.
22. *Manu*, VII, pp. 130-32.
23-24. *Śukra*, IV.ii, pp. 227-29.
25. *Epigraphia Indica*, XXI, p. 81, XX, p. 63.
26. S.K. Maity, *op. cit.*, p. 78.
27. Khoh plate of Yamātha, p. 122; Khoh plate of Sārbanātha, p. 129.
28. *Manu*, VII, pp. 128-29, 133.
29. *Fleet*, p. 254.
30. *Alina Plate of Śiladitya*, VIII.
31. *Fleet*.
32. Sircar, *Selected Inscriptions bearing on Indian History*, I, p. 372.
33. Bose, *Economy*, p. 126.
34. *Arthaśāstra*, II, p. 6.
35. Commentary of Bhattasvāmin — J.B.O.R.S. XI, pt. III, p. 83.
36. *Ghoshal's Historiography*, p. 172.
37-38. *Arthaśāstra*, II, pp. 24, 12.
39. S.K. Maity, *op. cit.*, p. 80.
40. *Manu*, VIII, p. 307.
41. S.K. Maity, *op. cit.*, p. 80.
42. *Raghuvaṁsa*, I, p. 45.

43. A.L. Basham, *op. cit.*, p. 108.
44. *Ibid.*, pp. 96-97.
45. Khoh plate of Sārbanātha, Khoh plate of Jayanātha.
46. *Arthaśāstra*, II, p. 6.
47. *Manu*, VIII, p. 307.
48-51. S.K. Maity, *op. cit.*, p. 82.
52. Khoh plate of Sārbanātha, Khoh plate of Jayanātha.
53. *Amarkoṣa*, pp. 3, 195.
54. H.R.S., pp. 4-5.
55-57. S.K. Maity, *op. cit.*, p. 83.
58. Jat I.I., p. 199.
59. *Milindāpānho*, p. 146.
60-63. S.K. Maity, *op. cit.*, p. 83.
64. *Fleet*, p. 98.
65. *H.R.S.*, p. 210.
66. S.K. Maity, *op. cit.*, p. 84.
67. Sircar, *op. cit.*, p. 371.
68. S.K. Maity, *op. cit.*, p. 85.
69. *Fleet*, pp. 97-98.
70. S.K. Maity, *op. cit.*, p. 85.
71. *H.R.S.*, p. 210.
72. Sircar, *op. cit.*, p. 371.
73. Stein's tr. of *Rājtarangini*, II, *op. cit.*, pp. 291-92.
74. Khoh copper plate, already cited.
75. *Fleet*, p. 196.
76. R.S. Sharma, *op. cit.*, p. 132.
77. S.K. Maity, *op. cit.*, p. 86.
78. *Fleet*, p. 166.
79. *Ibid.*, p. 179.
80. *Ibid.*, p. 173.
81. *H.R.S.*, p. 213.
82-83. S.K. Maity, *op. cit.*, p. 86.
84. *H.R.S.*, p. 213.
85. *Raghuvaṁsa*, I, pp. 75-91.
86. Khoh copper plate, already cited.
87. *Fleet*, p. 98.
88. *E.I.*, XII, p. 157.
89. *E.I.*, XI, p. 221.
90. *E.I.*, XII, p. 157.
91. *Harṣa-Charita*, VII.
92. S.K. Maity, *op. cit.*, p. 88.
93. A.L. Basham, *op. cit.*, p. 109.
94-98. *The Cultural Heritage*, Vol. II, p. 668.
99. *Ibid.*, pp. 668-69; *Kauṭilya*, Vol. 2, pp. 242-44; *Manu*, X, pp. 118-20.
100. *Patañjali*, IV, pp. 3, 99; A.L. Basham, *op. cit.*, p. 112.
101. *Kauṭilya*, Vol. 2, p. 246.
102-105. A.L. Basham, *op. cit.*, p. 105.
106. *Śukra*, I, pp. 315-17.
107. *Mānosallāsa*, II.4, pp. 439-40.
108-109. *The Cultural Heritage*, Vol. II, p. 669.

SELECT BIBLIOGRAPHY

Sanskrit Sources

B.K. Sarkar (tr.) : *Śukra-nītisāra*, Allahabad, 1914.
G. Būller (tr.) : *Laws of Manu*, Oxford, 1886.
G. Büller (tr.) : *Sacred Books of Aryas* (Dharamsala of Apastambha, Gautama, Vasistha and Baudhayana), Oxford, pp. 1879-82.
H. Kern : *Bṛhaspati-Saṁhita*, Calcultta, 1875.
H.D. Sharma and N.G. Sardesai (ed.) : *Amarkoṣa*, Poona, 1941.
J. Jolly (ed.) : *Narāda-Smṛti*, Calcutta, 1885.
J. Jolly (ed.) : *Viṣṇu-Smṛti*, Calcutta, 1881.
J.P. Vidyasagar (ed.) : *Kāmandakiya-Nīatisāra*, Calcutta, 1975.
M.A. Stein (ed.) : *Kalhana's Rājtaranginī*, Bombay, 1892.
N. Sastri and J. Sastri (ed.) : *Yājñavalkya-Smṛti*, Bombay, 1926.
P.C. Roy (ed.) : *Mahābhārata*, 7 volumes, Calcutta, 1887.
R.P. Kangle (Ed. and tr.) : *Kauṭilya's Arthaśāstra*, 3 volumes, Bombay, 1965.
R.D. Karmakar (ed.) : *Mṛcchakatika*, Poona, 1941.
S.C. Chakravorty : *Kālidasa Granthāvali*, Calcutta, 1916.

Greek Sources

J. Kennedy : "Early Commerce of Babylon and India," *JRAS*, 1898, 241ff.
J.W. McCrindle : *Ancient India as Described by Megasthenes and Arrain*, Calcutta, 1887.
J.W. McCrindle : *Ancient India as Described by Ptolemy*, 2nd Edition, (ed. by S.N. Majumdar), Calcutta, 1929.
J.W. McCrindle (tr.) : *Christian Topography of Cosmos*, London.
W. H. Schoff (tr.) : *The Periplus of the Erythrean Sea*, London, 1912.

Chinese Sources

James Legge (ed.) : *A Record of Buddhistic Kingdom by Fa-hien*, Oxford, 1886.

S. Beal (tr.) : *Life of Hiuen-tsang by Shamans Hwui Li and Yen Tsang*, 2nd edn., London, 1911.

T. Watters : *On Yuan Chawang's Travels in India*, 2 volumes, London, 1904-05.

Epigraphic Sources

Epigraphia Indica, published by the Government of India, Calcutta and Delhi.

Select Inscriptions Bearing on Indian History and Civilization by D.C. Sircar, Vol. I, Calcutta, 1942.

Inscriptions of the Early Gupta Kings and their Successors, edited by J.F. Fleet, London, 1888.

Inscriptions of Aśoka by E. Hultzsch, Oxford, 1925.

Books

A. Appadora : *Economic Conditions in South India*, 2 volumes, Madras, 1936.

A.S. Altekar : *Village Communities in Western India*, Oxford, 1921.

A.L. Basham : *The Wonder that was India*, London, 1954.

A.N. Bose : *Social and Rural Economy of Northern India*, 2 volumes, Calcutta, 1940-45.

B.C. Law : *Tribes in Ancient India*, Poona, 1943.

C.J. Brown : *The Coins of India*, Calcutta, 1922.

Debraj Chanana : *Slavery in Ancient India*, Delhi, 1960.

E.J. Rapson : *Ancient India*, Cambridge, 1916.

E.H. Warrington : *Commerce between the Roman Empire and India*, Cambridge, 1928.

G.H. Rawlinson : *Intercourse between India and the Western World*, Cambridge, 1916.

G.L. Adhya : *Economics of Early India* (C. 200 B.C. to A.D. 500), Bombay, 1965.

J.W. Rhys Davids (tr.) : *Questions of King Milinda*, Oxford, 1890, 1896.

J. Kennedy : "Early Commerce of Babylon and India", *J.R.A.S.*, 1898, 241ff.

L. Gopal : *Economic Life of Ancient India*, Delhi, 1965.

Pran Nath : *A Study in the Economic Conditions of Ancient India*, London, 1929.

Pran Nath : *Perspective in Social and Economic History of Ancient India*, New Delhi, 1983.

R. Choudhury : *An Economic History of Ancient India*, Patna, 1982.

R.C. Majumdar : *Ancient India*, 8th edn., Benaras, 1952.

R.C. Majumdar : *Corporate Life of Ancient India*, 2nd edn, Calcutta, 1922.

R.C. Majumdar and A.D. Pusalkar (ed.) : *The Vakataka-Gupta Age*, Lahore, 1946.

R.C. Majumdar and A.D. Pusalkar (ed.) : *The Classical Age*, 3rd edn., Bombay, 1954.

R.C. Majumdar and A.D. Pusalkar (ed.) : *The Age of Imperial Unity*, 2nd edn., Bombay, 1964.

R.C. Majumdar and A.D. Pusalkar (ed.) : *The Vedic Age*, 2nd edn., Bombay, 1964.

R.N. Salatore : *The Life in the Gupta Age*, Bombay, 1945.

R.S. Sharma : *Slavery in Ancient India*, Delhi, 1960.

R.S. Sharma : *Surdas in Ancient India*, Delhi, 1958.

R.S. Sharma : *Indian Feudalism*, Calcutta, 1965.

R.S. Sharma : *Perspective of Social and Economic History of Ancient India*, New Delhi, 1983.

R. Thapar : *Asoka and the Decline of the Maurya Empire*, Oxford, 1961.

Sir Paul Vinegradoff : *Outline of Historical Jurisprudence*, 2 volumes, Oxford, 1922.

S.K. Maity : *Economic Life of Northern India in the Gupta Period*, Calcutta, 1958.

S.K. Dey and others : *The Cultural Heritage of India*, 2nd edn., Calcutta, 1982, Vol. I & II.

U.N. Ghosal : *Contributions to the History of the Hindu Revenue System*, Calcutta, 1929.

U.N. Ghosal : *Agrarian System in Ancient India*, Calcutta, 1930.

U.N. Ghosal : *History of Hindu Public Life*, Calcutta, 1983.

U.N. Ghosal : *Hindu Revenue System*, Calcutta.

INDEX